RANDALL FRIEND was seeking spiritual answers for 30 years until he read Sri Nisargadatta Maharaj's book, *I Am That*. He eventually encountered 'Sailor' Bob Adamson and Gilbert Schultz. In this simple and uncompromising pointing, the search ended.

Randall holds weekly meetings as the avatar Avastu Maruti in *Second Life*, a 3D virtual world, where seekers from many countries come to hear the simple message of non-duality. Randall is the author of the blog *You Are Dreaming* (http://avastu0.blogspot.com), and has been featured in several episodes of *The Urban Guru Café* (http://urbanguru-cafe.com).

Randall resides in Louisville, Kentucky, USA.

You Are No Thing

∞

Recognizing Your True Nature

RANDALL FRIEND

NON-DUALITY PRESS

YOU ARE NO THING
First published May 2009 by Non-Duality Press

Typeset in Guardi 10.5/15 & ITC Stone Informal

Non-Duality Press | PO Box 2228 | Salisbury | SP2 2GZ
United Kingdom

ISBN: 978-0-9558290-7-9
www.non-dualitypress.com

To the beautiful appearance of my teachers, 'Sailor' Bob
Adamson and Gilbert Schultz, who are but brilliant
manifestations of this embracing Heart.

Contents

Part 3 – Your True Nature – the Self

Part 4 – Dialogues

Foreword

Throughout the dimensionless emptiness, throughout the timeless ages, Lights have appeared and continue to appear.

Lights attract moths, some from a great distance, some close by – some miss or do not recognize the Light at all and are attracted to reflections only and so keep on struggling...

Others basking in that Light are ignited by recognizing they are also and only that Light and rest as That. In resting, the steady Light, continually self-shining, cannot help but keep attracting effortlessly, and so it ever is.

Randall Friend is such a Light.

The beams or rays radiating from this book will reach vast distances, and bring those who have ears to hear and eyes to see – to recognize their true nature. As it was in the beginningless beginning is now and ever will be (now), One without a second.

Read Randall's book, contact him if necessary, and realize the Natural State that you always already are (that thou Art) – full stop.

'Sailor' Bob Adamson
Melbourne
September 2008

∞

One Essence expresses itself as everything–there are no exceptions. Some expressions appear to be clearer than others.

This book has obviously been written spontaneously from an intimate knowing presence, that is, in this case, called Randall.

If you read and ponder over what is offered in these pages, I am sure it will call forth a resonance in being. Recognition arises, because we already know it, because 'I am That–I am That by which I know I am'.

Understanding is silent–wordless.

Strangely enough, it seems that words themselves can reveal that silent understanding.

Gilbert Schultz
Melbourne
September 2008

Preface

The book is written in four parts.

Part 1 is from the perspective of the seeker and discusses the typical spiritual search and the tools we have been given, as well as the environment or location within which we undertake the spiritual path.

Part 2 talks about the teaching of Advaita Vedanta and other aspects of non-duality, finding our way out of suffering, finding the self, self-discovery or the dispelling of ignorance.

Part 3 points out our true nature – the vast and empty knowingness which pervades all, sees all, cannot be separated from the totality of present appearance.

Part 4 is a record of dialogues with readers. Despite mental analysis and thorough intellectual understanding, questions still come.

∞

This book is a simple repayment, a passing on of the courtesy, a manifestation of devotion, a compassion of sharing, an expression of the heart. This book is a container of worthless words acting only as a finger pointing to the moon.

This isn't a book about Advaita Vedanta or any of the other nondual traditions, as those are all only pointing to something beyond, something that a system or methodology or philosophy or religion could never contain.

Although some of the terms used may sound like spiri-tuality, nothing could be farther from the truth. What-you-truly-are has nothing to do with spirituality, nothing to do with religion, nothing to do with any thing, yet many of these words point to the same no thing.

The seeking mind uses analysis and conceptualization, which is useful in maintaining the survival of the organ-ism, yet helpless in understanding That which is beyond the mind.

Don't blindly accept anything that is contained in this or any other book. Don't add it to your already overloaded arsenal of beliefs. The point is that all beliefs are based on the false, they are only beliefs because we have no proof, no direct evidence to the contrary.

Heard through our ordinary framework of beliefs, this message is a paradox, fodder for endless argument.

Lay aside all preconceptions, beliefs, concepts. Don't take these words as any kind of gospel; sit back and see if they resonate, see if there might be some belief obscuring what's being said. Honestly look at what is being pointed to in this openness, let the message sink in without mental analysis. Don't try to figure it out.

The truth of what you are doesn't have to be figured out. You already are what you seek. We have to start from that fact. Nothing to find. Nothing to gain. No attaining or achieving, otherwise the mind is off on its path, off pursuing its goals.

The great spiritual search is nothing but a path lead-ing away from this moment, from now, even if we hear that we are already That. We gloss over it, sometimes subtly, sometimes overtly, in an attempt to *become*.

And if this is merely a passing interest, there is no compelling reason really to lay aside the concepts and beliefs through which we see the world. And filtered through concepts and beliefs, anything that is read or heard will be immediately analyzed within that framework, using that foundation.

But if there is a sincere and intense desire or earnestness to really know your true nature, the Oneness or true Self or God or whatever label you want to put on it, then an openness will arise. A helplessness in the face of hopelessness. An unlearning, a not-knowing.

∞

Much has been made of the differences in approaches within non-duality. Some say that nothing is necessary, that you are already That and no effort can ever make any difference, because the one who makes the effort is an illusion. Others say that effort is definitely required, that teachings must be applied and the student must be qualified by being open to seeing through beliefs.

My perspective is that both sides are correct. The first side takes an absolute stance, a hard-core stake-in-the-ground approach which, while being correct, can also be seen as not helpful. The other side takes the relative approach that as long as there is the appearance and belief that you are a human being and a seeker there is effort or investigation to be done.

It is clear that there is an appearance of a *me* that is suffering and seeking, looking for a way out, wanting a liberation or freedom that is, of course, already present. But until that is seen, the apparent seeker must do something and definitely appears to do something. This activity might include meditation or inquiry or a thousand other things. Something appears to take place.

We start with the idea of a *me* that is suffering and needs to find liberation, yet this liberation is not something we don't already have, not something we need to become.

In all of these seemingly split methodologies or non-methodologies it is clear that you are already That; you are already free now.

That is where we must start. Your true nature is already attained. You are no thing.

And this is the theme of this book.

Randall Friend
Louisville, Kentucky
September 2008

You Are No Thing

Part 1 – The Search

Bondage is when the mind longs for something, grieves about something, rejects something, holds on to something, is pleased about something or displeased about something.

- Ashtavakra Gita

A Summary of a Spiritual Search

How did Randall 'get' this? How did he realize this? How did he do this?

These questions are fundamentally meaningless, because they deal with a 'someone' who was never there, someone who never, for one moment, existed. They refer to a story and have nothing at all to do with finding out what you are.

They deal with a dream character, a fiction. They tell a story about 'getting' something, which is very clearly not the case. Nothing was seen, nothing was attained, nothing was achieved, nothing was added, nothing was changed.

It is simply a clear recognition of That which was already the case, already present, already fully and completely attained, which is to say that nothing at all was attained. It was clearly seen that the identification with Randall was an illusion, a mistaken identity, a belief in a dream.

The unmistakable truth about enlightenment is that there is no one there. There is no one who gets it, no one who could become it, no one who could ever reach it, find it, stumble upon it, realize it, attain it. There is no one there to be bathed in the light of God.

What you are is beyond even any idea of enlightenment.

This story isn't about someone gaining enlightenment or liberation. It's a story about the realization that there never was anyone, never was a person; not for one moment was there ever a Randall who was seeking or who could ever become enlightened.

1

Yet if this story points out the bumps in the road, if it resonates with familiarity, if it helps to weed out the contradictory myth of specialness, then it is appropriate.

∞

Once upon a time, 'Randall' was born into Christianity, dragged along to Sunday services and Vacation Bible School. It was the typical Christian upbringing, sipping and nibbling on the sacraments because lunch had been delayed, playing in the holy water, dreaming of sailboats and seagulls, wondering why everyone was so serious and uncomfortable in their Sunday best.

Yet this system of beliefs expected adherence, demanded faith, to the extent that anyone not exposed to its unquestionable truth was surely to burn in everlasting hell. To a young mind, this didn't make much sense.

At the time, alternative religions were seeping into the culture, hidden amongst the other taboos like his father's dirty magazines and stashed cans of beer. Meditation was also surfacing into public awareness, yet it originated from a foreign and far away place, the domain of the Devil and pot smokers, and definitely something a good Christian boy didn't want to take part in.

Maybe because of the disillusionment with Christianity, maybe just because it was taboo, Randall researched everything he could about meditation. Yet trying to sit still and still the mind was hard work.

Randall was fascinated by Buddhism, particularly the idea that a man could reach a state of enlightenment through meditation. Randall's young and fertile mind somehow equated this state with God

Many, many years seemed to pass; Randall found Buddhism a constant reading buddy, a way to take his mind off constant pressures and stress, an outlet for the suffering of a failed marriage and financial hardship.

Yet through these years, he had no real understanding, nothing came of it. Meditation was only a fascination, a way to calm down.

Randall's spiritual search continued, although it was little more than a bathing in alien words, reading a language which was not understood, pondering paradox with a keen intellect.

He explored many traditions: Zen, Taoism, Dzogchen. The idea that this was non-duality never once came to mind. Then Advaita Vedanta appeared.

Sri Nisargadatta Maharaj gave the first taste of Advaita Vedanta. Reading his book wasn't the typical spiritual fare, not the soft and fluffy new age hugs and flowers type of banter. Nisargadatta's message was like slamming your head into a brick wall as hard as you can. And once you got up, bleeding and semi-conscious, slamming it again and again.

All the trinkets and toys of the generic spiritual practice were shaken loose, called into question. The root of the great spiritual search was clearly, yet somehow obscenely, uncovered in all its glory and shame.

The Great Spiritual Search was really about becoming something different, something better. It was clearly understood that the lifetime of seeking was looking to the future, seeking a change, searching for something special.

This once-young man found that the internet had

become a reality, a far cry from the little available information on foreign philosophies from the library, or magazine subscriptions. Now Randall found 'Sailor' Bob Adamson and Gilbert Schultz available and present in cyberspace.

Randall exchanged emails with Gilbert, mostly with Randall expounding his vast intellectual abilities and skill at discernment. Gilbert repeatedly rejected even the most logical arguments with one recurring, uncompromising and annoying theme: 'Seeing is happening.'

Randall called on 'Sailor' Bob Adamson and found that Bob was as dear and kind as any human ever encountered. His message was clear: 'What you are seeking, you already are. You are no thing.'

After months of conversation with Gilbert and calls to Bob, Randall echoed many of the typical discourses of seeking. He had a clear intellectual understanding, but just wasn't there yet, hadn't seen This, was still missing a piece of the puzzle, needed something else. Then Randall found a talk by Bob on Gilbert's website:

'Well "knowing" is what I call intelligence. Not your intellect. Intelligence. That is the activity of knowing– intelligence energy. Knowing is an activity– of something that is going on in the immediacy of the moment. Any activity is a movement of energy. Not the content of knowing, I know this or I know that, that is all acquired, all conceptualized, all word stuff. The basic activity of knowing. You are not knowing a moment ago. You are not knowing a moment in the future either. It is going on in the immediacy of the moment, so it's an activity– something is happening now. It is this energy or life force or whatever label you want to put on it. It is functioning there in the immediacy of the moment. That is what you are.'

Something seemed to happen, fall apart, fall away. Nothing actually happened yet the identification as Randall was seen very clearly as false. The identification with the body-mind was seen to be a false assumption.

The belief in a person, a separate entity, a *me* bound and imprisoned in a body-mind was clearly recognized as merely belief, seen without the clouded filter of assumptions. The recognition was an opening, an allowing of truth to shine through. The overlay of belief fell apart in openness.

That clear, always and ever-present presence of knowing was recognized, realized to have always been there, noticed to be what *I am* and had always been.

Yes, seeing is happening. Without exception.

I really am no thing; not a thing, not an appearance, not the name and form, not a separate part, not a limited being. What-I-am is all of it, all that appears, all that comes and goes, all that arises and the open and spacious space in which it appears.

And in that, it is clear that it was never about achieving anything, never about becoming, never about 'only an intellectual understanding', never about 'almost there', never ever about 'I'm not there yet.' Only ever about recognizing That which was always there.

Recognizing the true nature as no thing.

That very freedom, that liberation, that peace, that love that was being sought, was already attained, always there. It was seemingly hidden but completely in full view, always.

The search was clearly and unmistakably over, not because all the answers were found or figured out but because the seeker, the person, was seen to be false, a fiction, non-existent.

I was no thing. Not a thing, not an appearance. Yet clearly this was already the case and had always been so.

The endless end of a beginningless beginning.

Our World

We have a shared view of the world. This view includes the commonly-held and scientifically proven belief in the big bang. And before that big bang there was apparently pure nothingness, nothing in existence, pure formless void.

Then the big bang happened – boom! Nothingness exploded into something; particles spread into this void, creating space, creating form, slowly spinning, creating gravitational pull, and gathering other particles together to form larger masses, asteroids, planets, suns and galaxies.

In this story of the big bang, the universe and all its content was created. And from those foundational substances all the rest was formed; the elements, compounds and molecules which led to the formation of cells. Eventually life sprang up, some sort of separate existence, the capacity for consciousness and the ability to know our existence.

With the coming of consciousness came the ability to know ourselves, to experience our existence. This means that we know that *we* are. Yet it seems that a false assumption has been made so that the story of creation is somehow backwards.

How can the universe, which wasn't originally endowed with the quality of knowing itself, suddenly create within itself, out of all these parts, the ability to look, to see? How can consciousness, a piece of the universe, suddenly be gifted with the ability to look up and know its origin, when that very universe has no ability to know?

That universe itself, which forms its parts from the whole, the totality of itself, must have the ability inherently to know its own creation, must contain this background of knowing for it to impart that to its creation.

That knowing of our existence hasn't sprung into being billions of years after the creation; that knowing is an inherent quality of the universe itself.

The universe is this very consciousness.

It seems that consciousness has a wonderful imagination.

∞

From this story we have our common view. We agree to believe it. We have no way of knowing for sure, outside of science's explanations and continual effort to prove that theory, to prove the truth of the story.

And here we live, on this planet, formed from the remnants of that booming beginning, springing up in different life forms, wandering in a world of separate beings.

And as a separate being, we're known as a person, a *someone* who somehow exists in this body, a finite existence, which itself was formed from the very elements of this original boom.

If we happen to be born into Christianity we are told that our essence is soul and that God caused this big bang or created the world for us, as separate beings, apart from Him yet created in His image. Our goal is to reach Him, to be like Him, so that we may, after the death of the body, be with Him, go to heaven, live in everlasting peace and paradise.

If we don't live up to the morals and regulations set down in this religion, we are doomed to hell, a place or condition which is so hideous, so awful, that we are totally scared into conforming, frightened into behavior of which God approves.

Here is this person, doing its best to live the right way, yet somehow not sure what exactly that means. We're not sure exactly what lies on the other side of death. We're constantly scared because we never really know if we're doing it right.

Yet this story holds a pointer to truth. It's the story of an original essence, a God, which has been seemingly broken up for the world to appear. It is a nothingness, a no-thing-ness, a void or original emptiness, out of which an explosion happened and then the appearance of the world was formed from various parts and pieces.

We might say that God or oneness had to be the same essence, had to be present, at that moment of universal conception. Whatever God or oneness is, whatever truth or reality is, it must have also been there for that event, long ago.

The common belief is that God is sitting outside of this creation, this universal space, this infinite playground; that He is somehow apart from, yet controlling every aspect, with power over all, seeing all, knowing all, omnipotent, omniscient and omnipresent.

It seems we conveniently ignore the omnipresent part.

Advaita Vedanta, and most religions (if we boil out the political and self-serving impurities added both in scripture and culture), point out that God is not somewhere outside, sitting on some golden throne, writing down each and every deed to be judged in a later day of reckoning.

God is omnipresent, present everywhere, present in everything. God can indeed be seen to be playing the world from inside, *as* the world, the very suchness or is-ness of the universe itself.

God is omnipotent, the very power or energy or activity of this world, this appearance, this universal substance. God or oneness or the Self is the very movement of the atom, the electron, the spinning of the planets, the pull of gravitation, the nuclear fields of the body, the DNA manifesting like the tree in the acorn.

God is omniscient, all knowing. The universe itself is suffused with the capacity to know itself, look at itself, appear to itself, through a million billion points of reference. Relativity is only an aspect of the absolute, only a seeing of itself like light broken up in a prism.

∞

Without the distractions of thought, without the distractions of body, without the distractions of planets and stars and pieces of this and that which came out of pure nothing, formed from emptiness; without these distractions we have an utter simplicity, an infinite potentiality of creation, of forms, of bodies and thoughts. An emptiness so full of potentiality that it burst in explosion with form, exploding an entire universe into being.

Whatever truth or reality is, it must have been there, before that big bang, the very essence of that boom, the very container and content of that original conception of the world we see and know and take to be made up of separate parts.

That very truth or reality must be here and now, must be the essence of what appears to be. That essence, that is-ness, that intelligence energy or formless void of infinite fullness, that must *be* the very essence of that body-mind that we've identified with.

Yet in identifying as a small, relative piece of this totality, of this infinite void of fullness, by identifying as a separate person, we've overlooked our infinite and eternal presence *as* the totality itself, as spaceless space, as formless form.

We've created a little character and a world to play in.

We couldn't have imagined a more believable story.

What Tools Do We Have?

Within this story, the tools we are given are this mind and this body. These tools are the only thing we have; nothing else is inherently ours. We can buy a shirt or shoes, a watch or a pair of glasses, but this body-mind, naked and without any attachments, is what we've been given.

And this body seems to be imperfect, constantly excreting waste or mucus, never quite conforming to our ideal of what it should be.

The body experiences menstruation, puberty, high cholesterol, blood pressure that is too low or too high, gains too much weight or is too skinny. It has beautiful hair and that hair turns grey and starts falling out. The skin is either too oily or too dry, so we must either moisturize or use acne medicine. The feet and the back ache, the prostate flares up, and migraines sometimes make it difficult to think clearly.

Oh, how we wish we had the body of an athlete or a professional dancer! Oh how we wish we had the health or beauty of an actor or an Olympian! The body is subjected to diets, cheap makeup, hair coloring or teeth whitening, all in a vain attempt to first of all make it presentable and hide the aging process, and to somehow prolong the lifespan.

Yet the body won't cooperate. The heart and arteries get full of the remnants of our poor diet, so that the heart has to work and work just to pump blood to the organs. That brain sometimes has deficiencies which cause all sorts of problems from headaches to psychoses.

And no matter what the body weighs, it's never right. It's too fat or too skinny. We buy up all the weight loss and exercise machines we can afford to literally work our asses off. The world requires us to fit into a nice picture of health and appearance, so when that pair of jeans starts to get snug, we are immediately thrown into panic, racing to the gym for three hours of working-out, immediately engaging in a crash diet or pure fasting, in order to fend off the impending obesity which we so dread.

Of course cells constantly die off, leaving unsightly dead skin, for which we must run to the salon for a pedicure. And this fact is glossed over, seen as an inconvenience, another problem which demands our attention.

But this cell death is an overlooked reality. Cells die. All of them. The body is nothing but cells – from the hair to the skin to the muscles, the heart and lungs and blood. All of these cells die, many at an alarmingly fast rate.

In fact, the entire body itself has died and replaced itself, through cell regeneration, many times over. The body you see when you look down or look in a mirror, is not the same body you saw yesterday or 5 years ago. It has replaced every single cell after a decade.

Even that original cell at conception, that combination of sperm and ovum, that original *me* was only a cell. And that cell has been dead for almost as long as you've been alive. That original cell was dead almost immediately, replaced and redoubled many times over during the nine months of gestation.

If we are this body, wouldn't we be found or located in that original cell?

It seems that we died before we were ever born.

∞

Yet the other tool we have been given is not much better. The mind is not always our friend. It is full of stuff that sometimes we'd prefer not to have. Thoughts come and they come and they come. Of course, since it's we ourselves that are doing it, that sets us right up for self-doubt, a lack of self-confidence and obsessive behaviors.

These thoughts seem to be what we are. They seem to be self-talk: *me* talking to myself. We are those thoughts, even though we can't seem to control them, even though they lead to words which sometimes don't seem to come out right, or contain embarrassing outbursts at just the wrong moment.

And in this mind we have memory. We can recall images of past experiences. We can remember our first date, our college graduation, and many other experiences we've had, including the really bad ones.

This mind also has imagination. We dream what the future might hold, creating a picture of what we'd like to happen, what might happen, what we're afraid might happen.

This back and forth between memory (the past) and imagination (the future) is what we do, most of the time. This pendulum of thought swings wildly, constantly. And this seemingly uncontrollable rollercoaster of mind is our experience of ourselves.

Yet mind is nothing other than a concept, a conceptual container in which we place thoughts, memories, imagination, mental pictures, songs which are heard on the radio and won't stop repeating.

Mind is only a word we've agreed to use to describe this process that is seemingly going on, yet that very word solidifies into a concept of something-that-exists, of something with independent or absolute existence. Something that stands on its own apart from the totality.

The mind is thought of as some thing, some place in the brain, some container in which this little person or soul resides and speaks from, like a radio announcer's booth.

Mind really means nothing, it's only a word. What it is used to describe is more the actuality, the experience of thought, the experience of memory, the experience of imagination, the pictures and images and various displays we know of as our mental world.

Yet mind has no substance, no actual existence.

So these are our tools. This is all we've been given as we make our entrance into this world, as we go through our life, as we try to make something of ourselves.

It's quite obvious, for those who might pause long enough to look, that we really have no idea what we are. We have no idea what we're even made of, or what the body-mind even is.

Yet without any investigation, without once even questioning these readily-available facts about the body, without slowing down long enough to notice, we're so sure it's 'my' body.

No wonder we suffer.

Suffering

We are suffering. It seems to be a universal law that suffering happens. We don't like what's going on. We want things to be different. We experience a loss, a loss of something we had, a loss of the opportunity to get something we wanted, a loss of someone we loved, a loss of our own health or beauty.

We don't like suffering. We want things. We need things. We desire these things which will make our lives better. We fear that we will lose our things.

If we don't get that job, we won't be able to pay our mortgage. If we don't get that new TV then that football game won't look as good when our friends come over. We must get that new car.

Yet there is something much deeper than these material desires. It is fear. Fear of death. Fear of losing. Fear of not being good enough. Fear of not possessing.

Identified as this body-mind, as this name and form, we are within this world, alien and separate. We are stuck with what we've been given, the limited tools which we strongly try to bend to our will.

We're determined to have a good life, have the things we want for ourselves and our children, rein in the forces of life to satisfy our demands, so that it's as we like it, as we need it. We're determined to *become* something better.

Yet life never complies. Life keeps on going, like a runaway train, in time. We can't move fast enough to keep up. We get an interview for that great job and find we have a new grey hair. We get that spot on the football team that we've worked so hard for only to bust our knee on the second snap. We get a date with a hot guy, only to have to cancel because our mother needs to go to the doctor.

Damn it! Why can't I be happy?! Why can't I have the things I want and need? Why does life put up so many roadblocks to my happiness? Why, just when everything was going so well, did he have to die? Why is life so cruel? Why is life so unjust? Why is this happening to *me*? Why can't my life be better?

Why, why, why?

And this, my friends, is the very essence of suffering. Trying to make life as we want it. Trying to have it our way. Trying to make *me* happy, often at the expense of others.

And it really never works out, at least not for long.

There's always something.

Me

It's all about *me*. It's all about my life. Every single thing we do is intended to be about me.

Even if we're compassionate, help a friend, give to charity or feed a homeless man, it's still, on some level, about *me*, what I did, what I get out of it, how it makes me look, how I feel about myself.

And if we love, it's always selfish love. It isn't love for the sake of that person. It is love for my sake, for what that person makes me feel like, for what happiness I get out of that relationship.

And this sort of love, if we can really call it love, is the source of jealousy, guilt, pride, fear. It is not unconditional love, which is loving no matter what, loving just because, loving without reason.

It's always with condition; as long as I am happy, as long as you are giving me what I need, then we love.

It isn't really love, is it? It's possession, attachment. It's absolute selfishness. It's fake love We are quite literally lying to ourselves, a tacit arrangement in which we allow that other person to be in our life, as long as they fit in with our nice little picture of ourselves and our life. As long as they make us happy.

∞

The life story, this fake love story, is a story about *me*. What I have gone through or done, what I am currently doing, what I will be doing or what might happen to me. What I can get out of life.

We're constantly trying to mold our life into what we want, taking pieces of the past, working hard to make the future better. There is always something about now that we don't like. There is always something about me-as-I-am that isn't good enough.

Yet the only thing we know about ourselves, that very definition of *me*, comes out of memory and imagination, is defined by our memories of that *me* in the past and what we imagine we might become. Becoming something better is our goal. Trying to fix our life is the constant yet sometimes hidden companion.

The tool we use is the capability of the mind to create a picture. We've created a picture of *me*. An image. When we think of *me* we recall this life story, this idea of *me*, this ideal of what we want this *me* to be, this insistence on a perfect me-story.

When we think of *me*, we imagine what this image might become, gather all our memories and imagination, which is all we ever have, and construct this idea of *me*.

Isn't that what *me* really is?

We know there is a body there, we know that thoughts are happening. We hear that name being called and this body-mind form responds We know that the vast collection of memories has always been about *me*, included *me*, included this body-mind.

This picture or image is what we're constantly trying to build, to construct, to shape, to mold into something we like while changing that which we don't.

We are somehow compelled to project this image constantly. If we feel our achievements haven't been fully recognized, we must assert this image and its accomplishments. If we feel this image is threatened, we push back with an eloquent description in order to properly adjust this image in the minds of others.

What we take ourselves to be is nothing but this image. This image might be called ego.

Sounds familiar?

And we mistakenly enter the spiritual search to kill this ego, to drop this separate person, to do something to make this sense of separation go away.

But separation never ever happened.

Realizing this is the real point of the spiritual search; realizing that there is no separate person to drop, no ego to kill.

The spiritual search is about realizing that the *me* is only a collection of memories and imagination, a story of combined desires and fears, a contraction of belief, a vague cloud of uncertainty, a glossing over of reality in the attempt to find a better reality.

It may be realized that there is no one to search, no one who can make things better, no separate life to improve, no *me* to become enlightened.

The *me* is simply imagination.

The Spiritual Search

So maybe after years of suffering, or just years of experiencing the impermanence of these image fixes, we turn to spirituality. We turn to the idea of becoming one with God or enlightenment or realization or liberation or oneness or some other term, the meaning of which we really don't know.

We read about this thing, this state called enlightenment, how it is pure bliss, pure freedom. We take pieces and parts from various sources and string together this imaginary picture of what enlightenment is, and that becomes our new goal. That becomes the imaginary picture of *me*. That is the template on which we will build our future, a future which will be filled with spiritual bliss and freedom.

Then our life will be better. Then this picture will be a good picture, full of love and happiness, full of wisdom. This picture will be of a *me* that never has any problems; everything will magically sort itself out in our enlightened presence.

I will know all, be all, be loved, be wanted, be needed. I will have the magical key to life. Then all my problems will be gone.

So this is a replacement for this fake love story, another way for me to be happy, another thing I can get, a state in which I won't need to find love, to maintain this farce that we know, deep down, is a farce.

Enlightenment, it seems to us, is a way out, an escape, a hope that there is some better place, some better state of mind, some way to happiness.

This is definitely seen as an attainment, something *I* will get, something *I* will become, something new, something different. Very different from my current, miserable life. It's an escape from the mild boredom and excruciating pain and fear that *I* currently experience.

But this isn't really what all the great sages have said. They have said that this enlightenment is not an attainment, not something you don't have already, not something you have to reach or find or get. It is something you're overlooking, something already attained, something fully present now that is seemingly missed, in preference for what might be.

But we don't want to hear that. We don't like *now*, whatever the hell it is. We don't want it to be about now, about something that is present. We don't want it to be about our true nature, because we feel that our true nature isn't good enough. We feel that we, as we currently stand, are not capable of freedom and bliss and peace and love.

We feel we already know our true nature, we've experienced it as that needling little guilt, as that suppressed jealousy over someone else's joy, as that hidden little pride when we're compassionate, as that faulty human being that really, honestly, doesn't know what the hell we're doing.

As that person, we are just trying desperately to juggle all the balls that life is throwing at us, feeling that we mostly are failing, feeling that no matter what we do, we're lost and separate in a somewhat violent and apathetic world.

That is what we want out of. That is what we don't want, to know our true nature. We desperately want something different, something better. We desperately want the peace that can only be found somewhere else, because peace is definitely not here, at least as we see it.

We want enlightenment to save us from ourselves. We want enlightenment to deliver the wisdom we feel we're lacking, the peace we so desperately desire, the love we can never get quite right.

But the message is consistent: your true nature is not this *me*, not this name and form, not this limited and grasping sense of self, not this idea of what you are. Your true nature is emptiness, full of form, knowing space, presence awareness, in which this limited and temporary name and form appear.

The message is very clear: you are already That, already enlightened, already free. What you are looking for is already here. So searching for it, as some event to come or state to reach, just doesn't make any sense.

Looking for it to arrive in a wonderful explosion of fireworks and bliss is an indication that we've overlooked or ignored the primary message which is you are already That.

But we don't really want to hear it, do we?

It seems that, in order to be delivered from this miserable life story, to be saved from it, we must really look at it. We must force our eyes upon the very tragedy and boredom and imperfection and insignificance which we feel actually describes our existence, our limited appearance in this vast and apathetic world.

Instead of ignoring it and hoping it will go away, it seems we must really look at it, we must notice it. It seems we must face the very thing we want to be rid of: the story of *me*.

∞

We go in search of this enlightenment. Many people seem to be getting a lot out of this enlightened person's books or meetings or website. We pick up the book which has the most positive reviews, we visit some websites, yet we aren't sure who really is enlightened. How the hell are we supposed to know? We dive in, we read, we listen, we spend endless hours listening to online videos or driving to satsangs. We sit there and listen, trying to figure out just what the hell they are saying.

We put out a lot of money on these books and pay to go to satsangs or retreats. This is another acquisition; it's going to cost some money. These gurus or teachers charge for the privilege of being in their presence. And, of course, this is the ultimate! You get what you pay for; that is our justification.

We compile all this knowledge: 'You are one with the Self, your true nature is bliss, look inside for the Guru'. We're not really sure what any of it means, but it sounds good. It sounds enlightened. So we just stick with it, analyze it like we do everything else and try to fit it nicely into this picture of me.

Yet we're left in our old, crappy life. We're left still not knowing what it's all about. We're left still seeking answers. We're eternally stuck in a mere intellectual understanding. We wonder why we keep on reading all this, listening to all this, wasting our time on all this.

We get very good with the spiritual language, the dressings and drippings of the spiritual life. Yet we still don't have it. We still aren't getting it. We still don't have that peace.

Maybe we begin a path. We start meditation. We start repeating mantras. We buy the right clothes and listen to all the right music, we start looking at how we can be more compassionate, more selfless. We try to be the witness. We try to see God in everything.

We try everything!

And in this trying, in this effort to become, in this habitual glossing over of the core of the message, to get that quick fix, that instant makeover, that enlightenment-in-10-easy-steps, we have already ensured that we will miss the point.

We have totally missed the fact that what we are seeking has been staring us in the face.

Our original face.

The face before we were born.

Resonation

Within the spiritual search, something resonates. Something makes sense. Something feels right. Something speaks to us, although we're not at all sure what it is.

This resonance with some of the messages encountered in our search somehow leads to a lessening of our fear, our continual grasping for the answer. We somehow, deep down, feel that what is being said is true, although we haven't become enlightened yet.

So we stick to the path, stay in meditation class or continue to pore through our library of spiritual books. We spend hours on the internet or at satsangs. We try and we try and we try to finally understand. The analytical mind is in overdrive, parsing out every word, looking for missed meanings, trying to find other possible meanings in each word uttered by the great gurus.

We feel we are so close. We really have a great intellectual understanding but we just aren't there yet. What is it? What the hell do I have to do to become enlightened? I've examined everything. I've looked everywhere. I've parsed every word, I've used every bit of knowledge I can get, I've done everything I know to do. I'm at the end of my rope!

At some point, we exhaust all our words, we run out of conceptual gas, we use up the mind until it becomes twisted like a hot pretzel in the mall. We are strung out on spirituality, still needing a fix but left without a direction, left with no more stones to turn over.

At some point, the mind stops trying.

The End of the Search

The previous chapters have described a typical spiritual search and the tools we've been given. There is a *me* that isn't happy with my life. There is a *me* that wants it to be different, wants to be happy, wants to end suffering.

Yet through all the efforts, we never reach what we are seeking. We never get enlightenment. So the great story has to end there, the search is doomed to fail, because enlightenment was never something we get, never something for the person to attain or achieve.

And even if this is clearly seen, then enlightenment is still never gained, because it is obvious that there is no one to become anything, including becoming enlightened.

But we've heard this before. It's just not convenient in our story, a story of *me*, suffering and seeking, looking yet not finding, wanting desperately to know the truth and reality of what-we-are.

We're looking to get out of this trap which we've created, this entanglement of uncertainty which we wade through, this murky idea about what-we-are.

But we've used our tools to capacity, applying our worldly knowledge as we've always done, exercising our belief system to its fullest. We have literally exhausted our capability to analyze these pointers, these spiritual messages, these paradoxical puzzles.

At some point we might be caught off guard, be shocked into silence, slam our head hard enough. We just might pause the search.

And in that pause we might, for the smallest fraction of a moment, look at what is going on, honestly look at the truth. In our frustration or exhaustion, we might be open to laying aside our shield of beliefs.

∞

Part 2 - Self-knowledge

This creation, which is a mere play of consciousness, rises up, like the delusion of a snake in a rope (when there is ignorance) and comes to an end when there is right knowledge.

-Yoga Vasishta

The *Me* Story

What really is this *me* we've taken ourselves to be? What is this person, this individual self, this tiny little speck in an enormous universe, wandering across a small planet, striving for things to make life better, unhappy at the things it doesn't like, having some moments of happiness but generally moments of sadness, despair, isolation, loneliness?

What really is this small self, this bundle of memories and imagination, this contraction against a hostile world, this sensation of being the center of whatever the hell we're stuck in?

This *me* is an idea, a concept. *Me* is a story, woven from the string of experiences gone by and the potential for experiences to come.

The *me* is an experience, formed entirely out of concepts, out of beliefs based on inattention to what's really going on, a mistake of perception, a creation of duality where none exists.

Me is a story of one who was born, yet that birth is also a story. The name and form was seemingly born, if we can even say that.

Any appearance is itself nothing other than an illusion, a gathering of perceptions and sensations and a placing of a label.

The person has no reality, no truth. The person is not there, never has been, never will be. Your true nature is not limited to name and form, not limited to abiding in a temporary and impermanent bag of skin.

31

Your true nature was present before the big bang, simply because the big bang is a concept which arises in this very illusion, the illusion that can never appear outside of this, this immediate moment.

You have created, out of experiences, the idea of *me*, the idea that you are limited and restricted, contracted and bound. You have imagined a character who desperately wants to be free of the prison of the *me*. You have constructed a dream of a separate life, lost and trying to find its way.

This *me*, this experience, this present sensation, this presence of knowing, cannot be separated from the grass, the breeze, the gentle waves lapping the shore.

You've simply forgotten that you were never bound, never restrained, never restricted, never limited, never subject to the violence of the subject/object equation, never limited by the mirage of duality.

You imagine a separate *me* and then look for a way to be free of that *me*. In remembering you were always free, always and already liberated, it is clear that this liberation is nothing more than the soft breeze blowing through the grass.

But, of course, these are only words.

Words

This section of the book talks about self-knowledge. Self-knowledge is knowing what you are, seeing the false as false, not this, not that. Self-knowledge is simply looking at our beliefs, examining our story, what we've been told or taught, what we've imagined, what we've blindly accepted as truth, and honestly seeing if it's true, if it holds up to investigation.

Self-knowledge is an honest evaluation of what we take ourselves to be, what we take the world to be. It is an inquiry into these default beliefs that are automatically handed out to our children, like a toolkit issued to soldiers marching into war.

Once children reach the stage where they can discern, where they can reason, where they can make a sentence, it is vital for them to use words if they are to function in this world. It is vital for them to know how to discern, to discriminate, to know the difference between an *I* and a chair.

And we teach them this reasoning, not because we know better and want to fool them. We teach them this simply because we don't know any better. We have fallen for the great story so we want to protect them, we want them to know the difference so they don't trip over that chair.

Self-knowledge is about honestly looking at these beliefs we hold so dear, so close, so tight; examining and discarding what is false. Not this, not that.

Yet we only know worldly knowledge. Worldly knowledge is something we strive for, something we gain in science or history or math or fashion design or computer programming. Worldly knowledge is acquired from the world we see, from the world we think we know.

Worldly knowledge has a commonly accepted and expected belief-system, something which is taboo to question. And this knowledge is something we want to attain, because then we will know the world. Then we will know what it's all about.

We use this crutch of knowledge to know the smallest of things, like a chair. Yet how do we know 'chair'? Where did we get that concept? We learned it from someone or somewhere. We learned that this thing is called a chair, just so that we would not trip over it.

But 'chair' is only a label. 'Chair' is not the thing-in-itself. 'Chair' doesn't really even describe that thing. We might say that thing is round or brown or blue, but 'chair' really doesn't mean anything.

And what about round or brown or blue? Do these words mean anything either? Do they actually describe that thing? What is the essence of that thing? How do we know that thing?

We sit on it. We trip over it. We experience it. We feel it is soft in some places and hard in others. We smell the aroma of wood, we see the curved lines.

Yet these are still words. We can't seem to get away from words in knowing that thing. What is soft? What is hard? What the hell do we really know about that thing that isn't a word?

Yet we do know it. We know the actuality of the thing.

Let's try another example:

We really know water. We shower in it, swim in it, drink with it, cook with it, water our lawns with it, get soaked with it on a spring day.

So what is water? Another word. Another label. Can the word 'water' quench your thirst? No, it is only the wetness or experience of that thing that quenches your thirst.

We start seeing that all of our words, the very foundation of our separate lives, the foundation of our world, are meaningless, relative, don't really describe anything. They only serve as communication. But we take them to be so much more.

We start seeing that the only way we truly know anything is through actual experience. We really only ever know what we're presently experiencing.

And then we add the commentary.

Self-knowledge is about looking deeply at what we take for granted as true, discovering how we've built our lives around these beliefs, these concepts. And discovering the inherent illusion, uncovering the real by seeing through the false. Words create a false reality.

A good example of this is the word 'time'.

Time

What is this thing called time? We seem to know it so well, like the back of our hand (or at least the version of time which appears on our wristwatch).

Yet upon close examination, upon laying aside our long-held and never-challenged beliefs for a moment, we see that time is a concept.

Wow! Time is a concept? Now that is a pretty big statement, because another foundation of our existence seems to be this thing called time. We need time to know when to show up for work, when to cook dinner, when to pick up our kids at school. We need time to know what time it is. And that's very important.

Yet time is a concept. It's conceptual. When can we experience anything? Can we experience yesterday? Five minutes ago? Tomorrow or five minutes from now? Can actual experience happen in the past or future? Or can it only happen now? In the present moment? In the immediacy of this very instant?

Can you experience that chair anytime outside of this moment?

We might have thoughts about yesterday or tomorrow, we might have thoughts about what happened or might happen, but those thoughts can only ever take place, be experienced, in the immediacy of this moment. *Now.*

This compulsion to go into the past and future in thought creates the illusion of time. We never go anywhere.

Those thoughts always happen in this very instant. They never happen any other time, except *now*.

'Now' really is a concept also, because if there is nowhere outside of now, does 'now' really mean anything? It's all now.

We have vast memories of our life and great imagination about the future, but without exception those memories or imaginings only arise, are only experienced, in this moment-without-a-second.

Take a moment to really see this, really feel this. Time is such an ingrained concept, so be open to the fact that you never really move in time. It is a false sensation, an habitual jumping from the past to the future, a compulsive mental movement from memory into imagination and back.

This very moment, this 'now', is like a container, holding the changes and measurements which we attribute to time, as if it were a thing-in-itself, as if it were some amazing scientific discovery, something we can hold in our hands, as if it were something real.

Stop – look – listen – smell – taste – feel. When can any of these perceptions occur? Not the memory, expectation, or imagination of what was seen, heard, smelled, tasted or felt but the actual perception itself.

And on top of the immediate and direct perceptions come thoughts about it, descriptions of the perception; the thoughts also are experienced right now, now, forever and ever now – as perceptions.

And if we stop for a moment, if we look directly at this moment, we may notice that this me-story is also appearing now. It is appearing as 'I am confused', or 'I am sitting here reading', or 'Yes, I understand that'.

This I-story is another experience, happening now.

The entire framework of beliefs, the great story of life, depends on time and requires time to exist.

It seems that no matter what appears in memory, or what appears in imagination, we can never get out of *now*.

Who Am I?

Throughout the spiritual search, we seem to be looking for something, some state, some experience, some confirmation of progress.

It is the typical goal-oriented mindset to put in effort and see results. Do this meditation or that sadhana, repeat this mantra or do that puja, all in the attempt at discovering the bliss or peace or wisdom promised by enlightenment.

Yet we constantly overlook the root question, the very foundation of the search itself. Who is doing the search? Who is doing the meditation or mantra? Who wants this bliss or peace? Who will be the recipient of this enlightenment?

Peripheral questions may arise in the search, the when, the where, the why, the how; yet the *who* is the very core question. *Who* does any of this apply to?

So the primary direction of the questioning is inward. Who is this me? Who is it that is suffering? Who is it that wants to end suffering? Who is it that needs bliss or peace?

Who am I?

This question focuses the mind upon one point, continually brings the mind back to the one central reference point which is the me-I-take-myself-to-be.

As the inevitable questions come up: 'How do I get this? What do I need to do? Where do I look?' as these typical vague inquiries arise, the direction is not to entertain the endless chatter but simply to ask who is asking the question.

Who am I?

As the thoughts come up and are noticed, the question naturally becomes 'To whom is the thought arising?'

As the questions about spiritual paths appear, the question effortlessly becomes 'Who will undergo these paths?'

It is a constant floodlight shone upon that ever-present but very subtle central reference point, that assumed self-center, who we've taken for granted as existing, taken on as identification without any investigation or questioning.

And it becomes very clear that most thoughts which come up, especially thoughts surrounding the spiritual search, are always referencing this *me*, this central reference point.

Who am I?

The thoughts point to someone, yet when turned around, when directed inward to find out who is being referenced, no one is ever found.

No-one can be located as a solid, separately existing entity. No one is present to receive the title *me*. No one sits, huddled inside that head, wired into the brain, ready to push all the right buttons, in command of this body-mind organism.

No one is found to be located behind that screen of self-reference. The only obvious thing present is this constant bundle of thought, this cloud of concepts and words, this knot of contraction which is quite obviously made up of beliefs and assumptions.

Yet as we gloss over the ramblings of the mind and the constant referencing to a non-existent entity called *me*, as we take for granted the very root or primary necessity for any of this search to be valid, we find ourselves wading in a pond of mud and murky water of our own inattention.

Who am I?

Who is it that has these thoughts? Who is it that is searching? Who is it that is the ultimate knower of all this? Who is it that is expected to find truth and reality?

∞

A light of awareness is shining, looking outward, assuming the presence of a looker, assuming the presence of a limited self who owns awareness, who is the projector of awareness.

This light is illuminating all that appears without effort. The totality of present appearance comes all at once – the room, the walls, the space, the desk, the book, the hands, the body, the breath, the heartbeat, the thoughts.

All these objects appear now, they arise within this ever-present light of awareness. Yet we consistently miss one vital point. Who is looking?

This question turns this light of awareness around to shine upon the one who is seeing all these objects. Yet in this illumination, in this flooding of light in the space where we're looking from, we find nothing at all.

We find no looker, no owner of awareness, no seer. We find nothing but darkness, silence, stillness, vast impersonal space.

We find no apparatus from which awareness is projected, from which awareness has its source. We find no mechanism performing the awareness, no limited space in which awareness functions.

We only find silence. Unidentified awareness. Formless

awareness. Vast, spacious and boundless awareness.

This boundlessness is almost a presence, a subtle feeling of existence, a simple feeling of being, a knowing presence which is very familiar, yet unidentified.

This presence isn't anything we can quantify, nothing we can measure. This presence of knowing doesn't have characteristics or attributes; it has no color, no shape, no size, no name, no form.

This knowing presence is vaguely familiar, as if it has been there all the time, underneath the identifications of appearance: a screen upon which the small self comes and goes, jumps around in play, asserts itself and then subsides.

This presence of awareness doesn't seem limited by the mind; the mind actually seems to appear on, or in, this very presence. The thoughts pop up and dissolve in the silence that is this very presence.

And these thoughts are the very mechanism in which this small self appears, the method by which the small self, the *me*, asserts itself.

These self-referencing thoughts are pointing to something which cannot be found, as the spotlight of awareness is directed within. These thoughts simply arise and point to something which is itself another thought, another belief, another assumption.

This assumption of who-I-am is what suffers. It is very clear that this knowing presence never suffers. This presence is the container in which the false suffering entity appears as only ever a thought.

Suffering is revealed to be another thought, another reference to this non-existent entity, another story about a fictional character.

Suffering is thought about a thought. Can a thought suffer? Can a thought be what-you-are?

To whom is the thought arising? Who is the knower of suffering thought?

And thought is seen, obviously, to be another experience, conceptualized and labeled as thought. The words themselves are somehow referencing something which is also another experience.

The *I* who I take myself to be is very clearly only known to arise as a thought, another experience.

Who is it that is doing the experiencing?

Direct Experience

We see that words are never the thing; words are not the thing-itself, only labels, only descriptions. We run around and around with words, trying to pin down what the thing is.

Yet we don't need words to know that thing. We don't need to describe it to know it. We don't need to label it. We already know it. It's here, now. It's This – just This.

The minute we label or describe This it becomes something conceptual, something meaningful, something separate, something existing in space and time. Yet we don't have to do that to know it. We simply experience it. And the only time we can experience it is now, in this moment, in the immediacy of this very instant.

We have a direct experience of that chair in this moment. We see it. We know it. And we can only see it and know it now. Pure experiencing is happening, right now.

This is what is meant by direct experience. We directly know or experience that thing, the only time we ever can, in this moment. We can't experience it yesterday or tomorrow. We can have thoughts about the experience, but not the direct experience itself.

Yet we compulsively miss this, because we need our words, they make us feel comfortable. We compulsively label our experiences. We overlook the direct and immediate experience-ing in preference for the idea, labels and concepts about it.

And in the very labeling, we actually create the idea that the thing is separate, we create the subject/object equation in this way. That thing is over there and I am here, I am seeing that chair. I am hearing that bird.

We use the word *I* to describe something that seems to be happening, a familiar body, a constant thinking, a general but vague sense of being a someone.

The words 'I' or 'I am' are like any other words, in that they are conceptual descriptions of an experience. These words are a translation of what-is-appearing, a conceptualization of direct experience.

The *I* points to the very experiencing itself. It points to the very knowing, the knowing of your existence. *I am* is a confirmation of this sense of presence, this presence of knowing, yet that presence gets mixed up with the body and thoughts; they get scrambled in with the very presence of that vast and clear space of perceiving.

So we say: 'I am hearing a bird'. We believe the story which is created by this describing, by this mental formulation, by this linguistic equation. We fall for the implication that there is actually someone hearing something. We are truly spellbound by words.

Yet the entire equation itself happens in experiencing, the entire thought-story about all this is another experience. Pure experiencing includes the thought-story about an *I* and a chair or a bird.

That seeing or that hearing is simply pure experiencing, pure see-ing and know-ing.

We can never know this, just what is happening now, just the totality of present appearance, using words and labels and descriptions and relative judgments based on these descriptions. And we never need to.

We are already effortlessly and eternally and purely experiencing whatever is happening, whatever appears. And the *me* that experiences also arises in that field of pure seeing.

Self-knowledge is about not blindly accepting the appearance of things, not blindly accepting the general beliefs about the world, but questioning, inquiring, looking into them.

The sages have said that the false casts a shadow over the real, a veil of illusion over the true.

We must dispel the false, dispel this ignorance which is like a veil over the true self, what we truly are.

Truth

What is truth? What is reality? When can these ever *be*? Can truth be something of tomorrow but not here and now? Can reality be something we gain or get or reach? Can it be something we attain?

No. Truth or reality must, if they are true and real, be something here, something now. Something must be here now for it to be true. It must be fully present for it to be reality. It can never be something that's yet to come, or has come and gone. It can't be here yet not have been present for the big bang. It couldn't have been present for the big bang and not be present now.

It can't be just a concept or a belief. Whatever it is, it must be always and ever present.

What is here and now? What is happening now that isn't temporary, that isn't coming and going, that isn't relative or impermanent? What is the very essence of what is happening now?

Isn't it that pure experiencing? The fact of experiencing? The fact that experiencing itself is happening? That which is experienced, and the experience-er, are both relative, descriptive, conceptual. The subject/object equation requires time to exist, requires belief to sustain, requires words and concepts to formulate.

Simply notice that pure experiencing is happening. Things happen, but without pure experiencing we would not know it. Thoughts come and go, but without pure experiencing we would not know it. That body seems to be there, doing all sorts of things, but without that pure experiencing, we would not know of a body.

This pure experiencing can only ever happen now, in the immediacy of this very instant. That is the only time and place that pure experiencing can happen.

Stop right now and see this.

And after this immediate pure experiencing, we go into thoughts to describe the content of pure experiencing, we create the subject/object equation in this conceptualization: that there is a *me* hearing a bird. We add on to the pure and naked experiencing by labeling and describing and judging and claiming ownership and *me*-ship.

Yet these conceptualizations, these labels are nothing more than thoughts. And these thoughts are another object arising in pure experiencing. Then we continue the analysis by labeling those thoughts good or bad, helpful or detrimental. We go deeper and deeper into abstraction in conceptualizing about the content of experiencing.

We may see that the content, the translated appearance, happens nowhere outside of this pure experiencing. It isn't the content, the mind, the thoughts, that are doing the seeing. It is the seeing in which the content itself arises.

What is happening? What is true? What is reality? Without relying on another experience to describe present experiencing, without using concepts to describe the conceptual, with a simple and honest openness, we see that pure experiencing, pure see-ing, pure know-ing, is all that we can really say is certain, all that we can be absolutely sure is real and true.

Simple looking. The fact of seeing. The presence of awareness. The obviousness and immediacy of pure experiencing.

48

The minute we begin to conceptualize, the minute we go into labels, the minute we open our mouths to talk about it or describe it or analyze it, that direct and immediate experiencing has passed, and the thought/word/speech has become the present content of *now*.

And we never, ever, need a word or a concept or a belief or time to know, to experience. That is already happening effortlessly, non-conceptually. That presence of seeing/knowing/experiencing is knowing the very idea of *me*, knowing the very idea of a world. Anything and everything we know of, conceive of, perceive, even the idea of an experiencer, happens in pure and naked experiencing.

Are you presently aware? Are you experiencing, right now? Whether thoughts are there or not, are you aware? Are you seeing? Are you knowing?

If the world appears as an experience, if that body appears as an experience, if those thoughts appear as an experience, yes, if even that very idea about what-you-are appears as an experience, then who is it that is experiencing? Who is the subject in this ultimate subject/object equation?

∞

Truth isn't something we find in relative words or concepts, simply because these are all arising in present experiencing, in pure seeing.

Truth isn't something we conceptualize, something we put together, something we make up or imagine.

Truth is a recognition or revelation of something that

is, something true, something real.

It is simply noticed. Discovered. Seen. It is simply recognized. Revealed to be already there, already true, already real.

Truth is wordless, pathless, objectless. Truth is the fact of being-the-experiencing itself.

The knowing that You are.

Knowing

Pure experience-ing is happening, without fail, without a doubt. It's obvious, if we stop and look.

The very fact that you're reading this indicates that experiencing is happening. You are experiencing the book, the words, the thoughts about the words, the room in which you're sitting, the sounds in the room, the sensations of sitting, the sensations of that body, the feel of the book in your hands, the breath, the heartbeat, the smells, the tastes.

On top of all this, the mind is labeling each one of these experiences. It is conceptualizing, using words, to describe these experiences. It is constantly doing this.

Know-ing is happening. That is the background on which, or in which, these experiences come and go. This knowing is the ground of each experience, the screen against which the things appear, the necessary foundation for the observation.

And even the *me* that seems to be the source of the experiencing is yet another idea in the experiencing, arising in awareness. How else can we know of a *me*? How else can we posit the idea that there is someone experiencing? Someone knowing? That concept arises as a thought, a story, and that is also experienced.

Can you get out of that experiencing? Can you know anything without it? Can you even know yourself without that presence of knowing?

We can talk about the brain doing this or the body doing that, the meaning of thoughts or the meaning of beliefs. But every single bit arises in experiencing. It is the experiencing itself that never changes, while all these appearances and thoughts and stories swirl around in impermanence, relativity, illusion.

What is left? Nothing at all. No Thing. Radiant knowing. Self-shining awareness. This is called knowing your Self. That is the light that illuminates the experiences.

It is not difficult. It is obvious, ever-present, always with you. That knowing/experiencing is the very stage on which this play of duality appears.

Experiencing is happening even now, as these words are read.

But even the sense of: 'I am reading a book' is conceptual.

An illusion.

Illusion

What is illusion? We hear over and over, It's all an illusion, it's all an illusion. But what does illusion really mean?

Illusion points to that which isn't what it seems to be, that which appears as something yet isn't really that. Illusion is like the mirage which seems to be water yet, upon investigation, is simply an optical illusion, simply a reflection of light.

Advaita Vedanta says that the world is an illusion. This world, this place in which we seem to live is an illusion. This constant appearance that we've seemingly been born into and from which we will die is an illusion. That to which we look for knowledge, that from which we gain all our attachments and material worth is an illusion. That in which we move around and exist is an illusion. The very place we seek within, looking to find reality and truth, is an illusion. This world, that we take as real without question, is an illusion.

Just like the mirage, it looks real. It seems like a world is there, with this body moving around in it. The sun rises and sets, the moon makes its appearance every night. The birds and the fish and the trees and the ants and the people are all moving around, seemingly contained within this world.

Yet, we must go back to the definition of illusion: that which seems real but isn't what it seems. The water in the mirage was real until we looked into it, until we investigated.

So let's investigate this world. Let's take a real, honest look at it. Let's put aside our beliefs for a time and just look. Anything is fair game, anything can be looked at. It doesn't have to be Advaita Vedanta or some other tradition, philosophy or religion. There is no spiritual rule that says we can't investigate outside of our chosen path. It can be science or rocks or fingerprints or excrement. It doesn't matter what it is: anything that helps is valid.

If the sages are right, then we should be able to just look at what is going on, we should be able to notice it, if we're looking with honesty, if we're not telling ourselves a story.

We don't really care about Advaita Vedanta or whatever it is. We just want the truth, we just want to know what we really are, we want to find out what is real and what is illusion.

Self-knowledge is not about just accepting what we're told, because that is exactly what we've always done. And once we've accepted a belief, we harden it against any threats. We contract if that belief is threatened or challenged.

Self-knowledge is about honesty, but it's also about seeing *how* we see. Seeing that we don't really pay attention to what we're doing. The world is illusion, not because it is some magical smoke and mirror trick, but because we simply don't notice reality.

Reality is staring us in the face. And we see this by simply examining our beliefs, by looking at how we look, by seeing how we see and deconstructing the beliefs that we've unquestionably taken on as real.

∞

Let's look at the brain itself, because this is seemingly where it all takes place. This is apparently the central head-quarters of the *me*, the place where perceptions happen, where awareness seems to come from. This is the place where consciousness seems to be located.

This idea that the self is located in the brain is native to the West; an eastern view is that the sense of self is located in the heart, or in the *hara* (the base of the abdomen). This feeling, which we in the West take to be fact, beyond ques-tion, is narrow cultural perspective.

This confusion on the real location of the self points to the fact that both are created in belief.

As we feel or believe it's in the brain, what is the brain? The brain is like a really fast computer, constantly pro-cessing input and making the body do what it has to do in order to live, generating thoughts, images, memory and imagination.

What are thoughts? If we look to the research on thoughts, to what thoughts really are, we find that they are neurons firing; millions and millions of neurons, firing in complex patterns at blinding speeds. And those signals are received within the brain and translated.

Are *you* making those neurons fire?

Are *you* pushing buttons from within the head at fright-ening speed in order to cause the neurons to fire in just the right sequence, like a video game which requires a complex combination of buttons? Are *you* controlling the millions of neurons necessary to make thought happen?

Are you?

Or is thought just happening? Aren't thoughts simply bubbling up? Aren't thoughts appearing? Have you ever had any control of thoughts?

Can *you* make a neuron fire?

Try it. Make a neuron fire now. Author a thought. Go on! You've been doing it all your life, haven't you? You are an expert at it, right?

Many of the problems we have are related to thought; we have good thoughts and bad thoughts. We try to change our thoughts, try to think more positively, try to react in a different way.

This all assumes control over thoughts, a control which was never really possible. It appears to be that way yet isn't what it seems.

Illusion.

∞

Another persistent symptom, another indication that we ignore direct reality, is the belief that we are the body. We reside *in* that body. We are somehow a person living in that body, some sort of soul or spirit confined in that container of skin and bone, blood and guts.

We accept this blindly, so much so that we miss exactly what the body really is. We miss the way we know the body.

We know the body because we see it. We feel it. We can smell it or touch it. The appearance of a body is determined by sensations and perceptions. We know of a body because we know these experiences, which we bundle up in a concept and call *body*.

If we don't conceptualize, then the body is nothing but a bundle of sensations, flowing and changing perceptions: the feeling we call feet, the feeling we call breathing, the feeling we call clothes against the skin, the appearance of hands and arms and torso and legs.

If we boil it down, drop the concept of a body, what's actually happening? What do we actually know? We know the sensations or perceptions of something. We know the various experiences that we conceptually bundle together and label as *body*.

That's it. That is what the body actually is. That is all we really know. Those sensations/perceptions are, without conceptualizing it, the extent of our knowledge about this thing we call *body*.

We have a perception, we experience a sensation, then we go into memory to compare that sensation to past sensations: 'Yes, that's my foot!'

Is there really a thing there, a body? How would you know, except for the stringing together of these sensations and perceptions? How would you know of a body or my body unless you depend on a concept?

∞

Let's look at another angle: this input that the brain processes is given by our senses. We have five senses: sight, smell, taste, touch and hearing. And these senses are how we know this world.

Take a moment to really let that sink in.

Our senses are the only way we know this world, which we've hypothesized as an illusion, which we've theorized as something out there, as we remain in here, as something which appears to be real but isn't.

57

The only way we can know this world is through these senses.

In order for this world to be real, our senses must be giving us accurate information. Our senses must be transmitting data to the brain on the exact makeup of the world, exactly as it is. Otherwise we would be receiving faulty information and we wouldn't know what's in front of us.

The very book you're holding, that is given to you through the senses, through the sense of sight, touch, maybe smell; you could even taste it if you wished. We rely on these senses to give us accurate information, to show us the world exactly as it really is.

We assume that we're looking directly out of the eyes, as if they were little windows to the outside world, as if they were clear panes of glass, as if we were on the inside of this head and the world were out there.

So let's look at the senses closely, let's look at what we know about the senses. Let's examine the eyes, the sense of sight.

We are seeing something, a book. Yet that something, that book is not perceived directly. Whatever that something is, it is seen because light hits it and is reflected to the eye. And the eye receives this light at the back of the eye, called the retina. And this retina gathers in the light, not the object itself, only the reflection in light. The eye gathers the light reflected and then compresses it to pure data, data which is passed back, as signals over nerves, to the brain.

And this process is the same for all other senses. The physical world is perceived through these senses and then compressed into data which is passed back to the brain.

The brain receives all this data, not an actual perception

or image or picture of the world, but data. Signals. Representations made by the senses, not actually what is there, what is seen directly, what is heard or smelled or tasted or touched.

It is a representation, a translation, not actually what's there.

And what does the brain do with this second-hand data? It takes it all, all the different pieces, and puts together a picture. A picture. What we're seeing is only a picture, a representation, a translation, of what's actually there, in front of us. We're not seeing what's actually there. We're seeing a picture.

A picture of hands holding a book.

Look, right now, at your hand. It's familiar. It seems real. It seems unquestionable. Yet are you really seeing a hand? Are you looking directly at it, or is it being represented? Is it appearing in its actuality, in its reality, or is it just a picture?

So this picture is generated from the information about the world, a translated image of what's there, a representation of what is, a picture of a world and a body living in it.

And we already know this picture; we call it consciousness.

In this picture of consciousness, we see everything. Everything we know appears in this picture. Everything we have ever known or experienced has been in this picture, has been a representation of the world received through the senses and displayed. We can't get out of it. We can't *know* in any way unless we experience it within the picture of consciousness.

We can go to the ends of the earth, to the farthest planet, to the deepest mine, to the depths of the ocean—

every single thing we see is appearing nowhere outside of this picture of consciousness.

Even the body appears in that picture. We see the body. We know the body. It appears in this picture. Raise your hand and it (whatever it is) appears to the eye as a reflection of light. That image is passed back to the brain and the brain creates a picture of a hand, in consciousness.

We see the legs, the torso, the feet, the chest, the arms. We can look in a mirror (still appearing in the picture of consciousness) and see the face, the head, the hair.

We see the world through these senses, and the senses are lying to us. The picture we see isn't an actual and direct perception of what's there. It is second-hand information, hearsay, it's stale.

The brain generates this picture, this moving panorama, this fantastic dream of clouds and cars, birds and break-ups, mountains and late mortgages.

It's a picture labeled consciousness.

The world is made up of consciousness.

∞

And we already know this. We know that picture, we know how that picture appears, we're intimately familiar with this picture, with this consciousness, because we see it at night when we're dreaming.

We go to sleep, we lie on our pillow. We don't move around, we don't get up in the middle of the night and do these activities, get chased by monsters, fall off cliffs. We don't actually go anywhere in our dreams, we simply lie there and watch the picture of consciousness unfold in dreams.

The world of dreamland seems authentic; we really believe we're there, when it's happening. We sometimes have to really question whether or not the dream actually happened.

We see ourselves in that dream, moving, acting, thinking, making decisions, working, interacting, running, being scared, having pleasure. Yet nothing really happened – it was only a dream.

That tool called *belief* was fully functioning while that dream was playing, while that picture was unfolding. That belief-system carried over into that dream, fooling us once again, making the false into the real.

The dream world is an illusion, precisely because it's not real, because it's only a picture happening in consciousness. That's why we know it's a dream, because we know it was only a picture happening in consciousness.

How is the waking state any different? We see the same picture of consciousness. We see the same character, and that character does the same thing in this picture, thinks, moves, acts, makes decisions, suffers.

Yet within the dream of the waking state, we believe it's different, we believe it is reality. We believe it. We assume it.

Yet if we look closely, with pure honesty, what's the difference?

Who is it that is aware of both the dream state and the waking state? Who is it that knows the coming and going of these pictures of consciousness?

The world is not out there with you in here. The world, the body, and the mind appear *in* this picture of consciousness, which is nothing other than an image, a conceptualized dream, an illusion.

There is no *out there*, and no *in here*. These distinctions are only conceptualizations based on faulty data, illusions generated by an assumption, taking a dream for reality.

Even the idea that consciousness is generated in the brain is an assumption, another story, gathered from the vast bank of knowledge available only in the illusion, the only place we have to look. In the picture itself, even the brain and the concept of consciousness are part of this appearing dream.

But we are fooled by consciousness, by that very picture, by the appearance. We're spellbound. We're caught in a dream from which we can't awake, seemingly trapped in an hallucination, a bad trip which won't wear off.

Yet this isn't actually a problem at all. Because we know it already – it's obvious. It's a tacit game, a Self which stands alone, as one, one-without-a-second.

It's a game we forgot we created. A treasure hunt in which we buried the map and forgot where to look.

It's a puzzle in which the clues are so obvious that they remain hidden, so close that they are overlooked, like looking for your lost car keys when they are right in your hand.

You seem to have lost your true Self, yet you are only playing a clever game. You are hiding from your Self in the most obvious place, you are simply hiding, by *being everything*.

Who is fooled? Who is imagining? Who watches this game being played? Who watches the world, the dream, the play of consciousness coming and going?

Prior to Consciousness

How do you know this picture? This picture of consciousness? How do you *know* it?

The picture itself appears, as an object. You must be the subject to that object, the witness of that object, the seer of that object. That picture appears to you. You know the picture, you know when it came this morning and you know it will disappear tonight. You fully know this. What-you-are knows it.

What-you-are knows the picture, yet isn't contained within the picture.

You can't be inside the picture or you wouldn't know of the picture, you wouldn't know it appeared and disappeared, you wouldn't see it come and go.

What-you-believe-yourself-to-be is what appears in the picture, in the dream. That person, that character, that *me*. This is the central reference point in that great story of 'my life'. That is what you've taken yourself to be. That is nothing more than an image appearing in an illusory picture which comes and goes, stops and starts.

The picture itself is formed from illusion, formed from a dependence on the second-hand and misleading mechanism of the senses.

Me is purely and simply a fiction. A fantasy. Imagination. Illusion.

The *me* has no actual substance; it is made of thought, appears only as a thought, as a concept, as a vague cloud of uncertainty, as a mental picture or image or ego or whatever label is used.

You, the real You, is prior to and beyond the picture of consciousness, aware of consciousness, which is the very picture of this relative appearance, this illusion we call the world.

You are there to see it when it comes, to watch it go, and You know of the absence of consciousness. You know the waking state, the dream state, and the deep dreamless state. You know these three states.

You are the witness to the appearance and disappearance of these three states.

What-you-are knows the coming and going of all states. Any state can never be what-you-are, even a state of enlightenment.

All states are temporary; what-you-are sees all states and is the necessary principle for any state to arise.

What-you-are is That on which this name has come, on which this form has come. What-you-are is That on which this world has come, this very picture of consciousness, this dream of *me*.

What-you-are is That which can never be forgotten, so never needs remembering. What-you-are is That in which the mind appears, trying to remember what-you-are.

Of course, if we stay with the accepted belief structure, if we continue playing this game, telling this story, this is totally a paradox, because we believe we are this small little me-person, trapped in this body, which appears in this room, in this house, and that house appears on this planet, and this planet appears in the universe.

And the universe is some vast, open space, allowing all that appears to be, to come and go. The universe seems to be the container of it all, is the very source of these parts, yet the universe is somehow the totality of all of it.

Infinity. Eternity. Vast No-Thing-ness. Void.

You are the universe, the totality, the Self.

What is your original face? The face before you were born? What were you before the big bang? Before the universe itself appeared?

What does the universe itself appear *in*?

It appears in you.

What-you-are.

No thing.

You Know I AM

Advaita Vedanta calls this recognizing your true nature simply because you already know it. You already are that. You know *I am,* you know that you are. That is undeniable, obvious. You know it.

Although it is repeated over and over, read time and time again, the mind cannot accept it. The mind doesn't want it to be about what already is, what is already present. The mind wants it to be something better, something different.

Yet this is what seems to be the obscuring factor: the idea that what is, here and now, is not good enough, too simple, too boring, too ordinary. The content of *now* is what we're trying to get out of, rather than what we're trying to rest in.

But as long as we yearn for something else, as long as we desire something more, we will forever miss what is being pointed out.

When we come to the point where all words fail, all concepts fall short, all ideas about what-we-are get exhausted; once we have driven the search into a brick wall, smoking and crushed like a tin can, we are left with no direction, nowhere to turn, nowhere else to draw spiritual concepts from. We are only hearing the same message, being repeated over and over and over.

The mind is left without any fuel, without anything to grip, no foothold, no traction. It literally has nowhere left to look, no more satisfaction is gained from simply playing with concepts.

There is no more fun in toying around with enlightenment, wishing it would come, expecting these bright lights
and fireworks, levitations, miracles, flowing robes and
beards; these concepts have all become ridiculous examples
of peripheral grazing on the myth of enlightenment.

We are sunk deep, lost without a compass, unable to see
the world in quite the same way. We are buried somewhere
and not sure how to dig our way out.

So we simply stop. We rest. We take a deep breath,
allowing all possibilities to arise, opening the armored gates
of belief to swing free, gently relaxing that contraction of
fear; we accept the possibility that what-I-am is nothing
perceivable, nothing conceivable, nothing at all know-able.

We give up the fantasies of the future and we simply
look at this very moment.

∞

Who is reading this book? You say: 'I am. I am reading this
book.'

How do you know you are reading this book? Where
did this idea come from? How is it that you know this?

There seems to be a book there, hands holding it, being
seen through eyes, the words and language are known, the
mind translates, and there is a sense of conceptualization
of the message.

It's very obvious, if we dare to look, that this entire
experience of *me* reading a book is nothing but a sensation, a bundle of perception, a conceptualization of what's
known, of what's arising, of what's appearing to happen.

Yet that wasn't the question.

Who is reading this book? Who? We've only described a body-mind, a name and form. We've only described the appearance, again.

Who is it reading this book? It can't be that name, because that name is relative. That name was decided, it's completely arbitrary. That name can't be your true essence.

Who is reading this book? It can't be that body. That body is impermanent, formed from cells, made up of food, a flowing current of water, vegetables, beef, air, energy. That body doesn't have, as its nature, simply what the eyes can see, what the senses deliver. That body is only the result of the cells, the plants and animals, the very universe itself.

That body can't be who is reading this book. That name and form can't be what you are. If we look closely enough, we realize that what-I-am is seeing that body, seeing that body reading a book.

So, who is reading the book? There seems to be someone reading. There seems to be somebody reading a book. There seems to be a subject seeing an object. Yet that somebody is an idea appearing in knowing. That something, the book, is an object in appearance, arising in knowing.

So who is it? Who is doing the seeing?

Something is appearing to happen; that book is appearing, that body is appearing, these words are appearing. Thoughts about the words are appearing. The idea of 'I am reading the book' is appearing.

If we're honest enough, it is noticed that thoughts are also appearing in this very same knowing, this immediate experiencing. This pure and instantaneous, effortless awareness.

We only know these things as immediate sensations, instantaneous and effortless vibrations appearing, and this appearing is happening without thought, without conceptualization, without any ideas or labels placed on it.

I am reading the book. I am reading. I am. I know I am, I exist. Existence is the factor, the knowing, the principle which makes it impossible to deny that I am, the very principle necessary before anything else can be known.

And what is this *I am*? It is the knowledge that you are, that you exist. It is that principle that you are intimately familiar with; it's closer than your face, your breath, closer than thoughts or feelings.

There is something present. Presence. The presence of knowing, knowing that you are. That is not some thing appearing, not some image or vague cloud of uncertainty.

That is not any thing, because things appear in this presence of what you are. Any appearance makes its rising and setting within this vast knowing-that-you-are.

That knowing-that-you-are is fully evident, fully attained, fully present; you are aware of your existence, this knowing that you know. And it is this very knowing-that-you-are which is necessary for anything else to be known, for anything else to appear. It is this knowing-that-you-are which is the very container in which this body-mind-world appears.

Yet the ultimate knower never appears, can never be known as an appearance, as another object. We can never get behind that knowing, yet we know, yet we are the ultimate knower to all things known.

It is like the Zen saying: You must feel as if you hold a hot iron ball in your mouth, which you can neither swallow nor spit out, you cannot negate it, you cannot spit it out, yet it *is*, it is present, it is *presence*.

69

We cannot separate the burning ball of iron from the tongue being burned, from the *me* that needs to either swallow or spit. The entire subject/object equation is irrelevant in that moment of burning-ball-tongue-me.

As with the hot iron ball, you cannot deny this immediate knowing presence, yet you cannot see it. You cannot find it, yet it's obvious. Like the hot iron ball, it is immediate, suffusing all experience with the quality of knowing, not something that comes and goes, not something that gets forgotten or needs to be remembered.

It is you – This – this immediate and effortless knowing that you are.

You know that *I am*. Any thing we use to define that *I am* is not it. Any idea we have about that *I am* is not it. Any concept we have or word we use to describe that *I am* is not it.

It is the sense of *I am* prior to the thought 'I am'. The mind simply translates that sense of presence, that presence of knowing, into the words 'I am' and that is then identified with the body-mind.

You are not, yet *You* are. The limited self, that impermanent name and form you have taken your Self to be, is not what *you* are. The timeless, spaceless knowing presence, in which the concept and appearance of time and space appears, That which can never be seen, heard, felt, tasted, smelled or touched – *is*.

The very seeing, hearing, feeling, tasting, smelling and touching, the pure no thing which is nothing other than experiencing itself, is You.

That *I am*, that which can never be a subjective and separate experience-er, can never be the object of experience, can never be known, yet can never, ever, be denied.

The End of Suffering

It is only a *me* who can suffer, a *me* who can lose, a *me* who doesn't have what I need or wants more than I have.

It is only a restricted self-center who needs to be happy, who wants to avoid pain, who desperately and in vain seeks for a way out of this suffering existence.

The world and the one living in it are stories. And this great story includes one who suffers, one who is happy, one who is seeking, and one who might find or attain enlightenment.

There is literally nothing that needs to be done with the *me* because that very *me* is a fiction, an illusion, a false story which never ever had any basis in reality, in truth.

The *me* has no substance, no independent nature, no reality, no truth. The *me* is a mistaken notion, founded in innocence and unknowingly identified with.

The *me* is a false paradigm upon which we base every single idea, opinion, belief, desire, fear.

The *me* is a kaleidoscope through which we see a separate world, a filter through which we gather only that which seems to fit, while discarding the rest.

No place can be visited, no teacher can be learned from, no book can be read, no method or practice can ultimately make any difference because the root of the entire issue is the *me* that does any of this, needs any of this.

The *me* is the central character in this story that never happened. It only appeared to.

You have always been there to see it come and go.

71

Part 3 – Your True Nature—the Self

*Just as the ocean is nothing but water, the entire world of things
is nothing but Consciousness filling all the quarters like
the infinite space.*

- Yoga Vasishta

The Witness

Look now. The world appears. You see it. You know it. It appears as an object. You are the pure witness of that object. It arises effortlessly, is experienced effortlessly in this awareness. So you are not that world.

Look now. The body appears. You see it. You know it. It appears as various sensations, the warmth or the chill, the sensation of breathing, of heart-beating. It appears as an object. You are the pure witness of that object, of that bundle of ever-changing sensations. The body is an experience to that witness. The body arises in awareness. So you are not that body.

Look now. Thoughts appear. You know the thoughts. You see them come and go, rising and disappearing, providing the color, content and commentary with descriptions of the world, concepts and beliefs. These are all content of thought, which is itself an appearance, an object to that pure witnessing, that present awareness. Thoughts are experienced effortlessly in this awareness. So you are not those thoughts.

And in thought, the idea of *me* arises, the belief in a person comes. In thought, we label and describe present experience, seemingly separating out the solid block of appearance into things, into this and that.

Thought is the filter, the tool which we use to know the world, a continual reference to words, knowledge and concepts, out of which we pull references for everything.

Look now. All these things are only conceptual combinations of passing sensations, impermanent perceptions, experiences which we've bundled together to create the idea of world, body, thoughts; labels which we've taken to be real.

In fact, we can't know anything unless we label it, describe it, call it something. And in calling it something, we assume its separateness. If we call that a chair, we assume all else that is not-chair. We create the very dualism of opposites, we create the very subject/object equation in thought.

We create the idea of *me* in thought. This thought-belief or thought-story appears in thought. How else would we know of a *me*? This knowledge that we can gain or learn is the substance of the me-thought.

And it's very clear, if we're open to looking, that the me-thought is just a thought, just another appearance, appearing to that pure witnessing, that present awareness.

It's very clear, if we lay aside our strongly-held beliefs, that the *me* is only ever an idea, yet what you are is beyond, watching these thoughts come and go. It's obvious that this is the case, yet those thoughts, that filter, seemingly obscure this.

Yet nothing really obscures; the light of this witness shines and illuminates the very thought which seems to obscure.

You are simply that pure witness, watching the world, the body, and the thoughts come and go.

Can you watch the watching? Can you see the seeing?

Interdependence

All things exist only because of other things.

You are reading a book. That book is made of paper. That paper would not exist were it not for trees. The trees would not exist without sunshine, soil, rain. The rain would not exist without moisture in the air, clouds, changing temperatures.

Take any one of these factors out and that book would not exist. That book is the sunshine itself, the soil, the rain, the clouds.

And the basis for all of this to appear is space; space is the essence of form, that which surrounds form, that which is necessary for the form to exist. And space/form mutually arise, they are inseparable. Try to have a form without space.

Space is the very container in which form exists. The very book you're holding is nothing but the sunshine, the earth, space.

And that body, which holds the book, also has dependence on its very existence because of these same elements.

In fact, that body is nothing but these elements.

The sun and the soil and the rain combine to create the grass and the vegetables. Cows eat the grass and they are slaughtered for meat. The grandparents eat the meat and vegetables and the body converts that food to cells, muscles, blood, bone.

The bodies of your grandparents are nothing but this

food, this sunshine and soil and rain, cows and grass and vegetables.

The bodies of your grandparents combined by sharing their cells, those cells which are nothing but the sunshine and soil and rain, cows and grass and vegetables. The sperm and ovum merged and that original cell grew and replicated itself, doubled and tripled. It sprouted arms and legs and eyes and a brain.

And that little body was nothing more than the sun and the soil and the rain, the cows and the grass and the vegetables.

Without any one of these, that little body would not exist, would not appear.

That body grew up and combined with another, shared cells in the same fashion, and then you were born, upright and proper, taking yourself to be independent from the sun, which is present in all things; taking yourself to be separate from the grass, which you take for granted as you step on it or mow it; taking yourself to be separate from the cows and the vegetables, the soil and the rain, on which your very existence depends, the existence of that body which you so proudly call your own.

And the sun and the soil and the rain, the cows and the grass and the vegetables, all these are dependent on that livingness, that intelligence from which they are formed, those atomic reactions, that quantum mystery, that vast emptiness which appears to be solid, formed, substantial, even separate.

Every single bit of what you call the world is interdependent. One part simply cannot exist without the whole, without the totality, without that intelligence. That intelligence which is not outside of or acting upon, not some supreme lord sitting behind pearly gates and upon a throne of clouds. But that Intelligence which is nothing other than the sun itself, the soil itself, the rain and the cows and the grass.

And as that body begins to crumble, begins the slow decline we call aging and death, as that body breathes in the last gasp of air, air which is in essence the very same substance as that body, as this happens life is in the process of creation, of feeding itself, of changing itself in a continual evolution of rising and falling formations, formations which, at their core, are the very same substance.

So the heart stops, the lungs exhale for the very last time, a few words are said in remembrance, and that body is disposed of, waiting to decay.

Yet life is one – one substance. That body, which is nothing but life, continues on its journey, as food for bacteria and maggots, as fertilizer for the soil, for the trees, as a source of renewal for this one life, in its many appearances.

Nothing is lost, nothing dies. Life carries on, through life.

The essence is life.

As appearances, we take these things to be separate, we conceptualize that they are standing alone, existing separately, that they have their own independent nature and substance.

If we begin to see the gross ignorance, enormous pretention and subtle violence that is indicated by our insistence on separation, if we simply take an honest look, we realize that life is living itself.

As we step outside into the fresh air, as we look around at the trees and the birds, the cars and the pollution, the flowers and the bees, the cows and the shoes, the cigarettes and cancer, as we look deeply at what is appearing, we may notice something staring us in the face. We may realize that everywhere we turn, *life is*. Anywhere we go, *life is*.

The very body, formed from the sun and the soil, itself is life, itself is nothing other than that one substance, that intelligence, that knowing presence, that form from emptiness.

It may hit us like a ton of bricks, or tap us gently on the shoulder.

Life is looking at itself. Life is experiencing itself. Life is knowing itself.

You knowing that You are.

Which really means that there is nothing outside of life, nothing doing the experiencing, nothing to be experienced.

Nothing coming, nothing going.

Just pure experiencing.

Experience vs. Experiencing

What is an experience? We have to describe it to say. We have to use words to speak about it. We have to create the subject/object equation to be able to communicate it.

'I am hearing a bird.' That's a common experience. We all know what that means. We can relate to or identify with that experience.

Yet what are we really talking about? When is that experience happening? The moment we quantify it, it's gone. The moment we talk about it, it's conceptual. The moment we split up the immediacy of this moment, we've created separation, we've created the subject/object equation.

'I am hearing a bird.' This assumes the reality of an *I* who is capable of hearing, through senses, from within a body observing an outside world, where a bird is doing something, singing, making a noise.

This involves layers of illusion. Layers of assumption. layers of belief. Yet this is our reality. This is the language with which we communicate our experiences.

We've invented an *I* who is hearing a bird, but all we really know for sure is that hearing is happening. Experiencing. Pure naked experiencing is happening, in the immediacy of this very moment.

Whatever it is, we really don't know. We really don't know about an *I* who is hearing or a bird that sings. We only really, truly know that hearing is happening, pure experiencing.

Yet we must describe it in some terms. We can't say anything about pure experiencing. We can't describe it without words. In the process of description, there has to be someone doing the hearing, capable of hearing, the receiver of the sound, a subject. And it seems there has to be some object making the sound, transmitting the sound.

In thought/belief, in imagination, we take this entire equation for granted. We just blindly accept the situation as we believe it, as it seems to be.

We believe that the conceptualization of a subject *I* that is hearing an object *bird* actually points to a reality that is of separate existences, of an *I* and of birds.

Yet, in reality, there is no *I* hearing a bird and no bird, no song. There is only the hearing, only the seeing, only pure naked experiencing.

The *I* and the bird are conventions of language, convenient conceptual distinctions. Nothing more.

No *I* and no bird.

All sensations and perceptions appear on this pure experiencing, so much so that we can't distinguish the experiencing from the experience.

No center. No boundary. Totality is This here now, non-conceptual, pure experiencing which contains both ideas of subject and object. Pure knowing which sees the thought in which this illusion is seemingly created.

Just life.

Just This.

The Cliff

We see the falseness of words, the illusion of time, the veil of the world. We recognize the fallacy and impermanence of this great story of life we've constructed, built on belief. And as we see these, as we get a glimpse of the very mechanism of identification with the false – we're ejected, we fall, we lose our grasp.

We lose the very foundation of what we've held so dear. We move closer and closer to the edge of the cliff, as we clearly see the lack of truth and reality in our concepts of ourselves and the world.

We stand, balancing between grasping and falling, toeing the line between the hard ground of existence-as-we-know-it and total death. We fear a slight breeze might sweep us into abject void, pure and endless nothingness, loss of family and career and worth and wealth, loss of meaning, loss of hope, loss of love, loss of everything.

Yet we can no longer believe that anything is to be added, nothing is-as-it-seems, nothing persists, nothing is real, nothing is true. We can no longer believe these very eyes; the images we see come and go are no longer trusted.

Every perception we have is immediate. We can no longer sweep away our boredom by ruminating on the past or fantasizing about some wonderful future.

Words become a splash of illusion, building blocks for this dream which is falling apart. Beliefs become the opaque curtain which seems to obscure that-in-which the illusion plays its game.

We're lost; our maps have been taken, our compass has been crushed into a million pieces. The sun, which would provide us a sense of direction, is no longer a capable guide, no longer a separate beacon to which we look.

Because the sun, what we believed was our warmth and life-giving source, is very clearly not out there, but in-here, rising and setting within our heart-of-hearts. The galaxies so far away are somehow spinning within our own Self. The universe, that child of nothingness, that offspring of void, that formation of pure and simple emptiness, the universe itself simply cannot exist without our presence.

So we fall. Not because we choose to, not because we've run out of ground, not because we slip or stumble, but simply because we clearly see that the very ground upon which we stand is illusion. We see that the dream character which was clinging to the edge has no separate existence, has no reality and never, ever, for one moment, existed.

We fall back into our true Self, That which we've never left, That which we truly are. We fall but there is nowhere to land, nowhere to go. There is nowhere outside of our Self to end up.

We rest in our beingness, That in which this relative world comes and goes, That from which we create the impermanent world, That which is the universe itself, the limitless container which is evident in the swaying trees, the ripples of water, the pull of the sun, the beating of the heart.

You are NOT

The *me*, the *I*, the person we take ourselves to be, can only ever be an experience, something arising, something appearing, as a thought, as a story, as a belief, as an image, as a picture, as a reference point, as a supposed center of what seems to be happening.

That *me* that you believe yourself to be is something happening, something seen, something known, something appearing, some thing.

Yet any thing has its beginning and its end. Any thing is quantifiable, measurable, knowable, feel-able.

But the very essence, the very nature, the very source of all of this, is pure naked luminous and obvious experiencing, seeing/knowing, be-ing. That which isn't a thing, that which can never be quantified, qualified, measured, named, known, felt, seen, heard, tasted, smelled. That which requires no beginning or end, no time, no space, no individuality, no personality, no state, no lack of state.

The very seeing itself. The very knowing itself. The very fact of experiencing.

Emptiness, full of form, pure intelligence, no-thing-ness, pure and simple witnessing presence, seeing oneness, life living itself, experiencing absence.

One-without-a-second.

And even the idea of one or oneness or enlightenment or God or the Self dissolves back into the silent and still presence of no-thing-ness, makes its departure from the dream of becoming, bows out as pure concept, as does the small one, the *me*, who might ever find or attain or meet or reach or become one with God or oneness.

That sense of knowing gets translated through the mind as *I am*, as a separate person that is, that exists independently. That you, that concept of *I am,* is not, is non-existent, a fiction, a falsehood. This person is a story-of-stories, the central character in the dream of my life, in the great story of *me*.

Enlightenment has been called the great annihilation. It's an annihilation, not because there was something and now it's gone, not because there was a *me* there but now it's gone, dissolved, done away with; but because there never was anyone there. Even the recognition of this, which can only ever be now, is annihilated as only applying to some-one who never existed.

You are no thing.

Not-Finding, Not-Knowing

There is nowhere to go. There is nothing to do. Nothing to find, nothing to get, nothing to attain.

Words are meaningless. No word is it. No concept is it. No question can ever find it. No answer can ever be given that is accurate.

The world we see and believe that we live in is an illusion and anything found or gained within that illusion is more illusion. There is literally nowhere within this appearance to go.

The Great Search is a search for answers, for peace, within the illusion, within the dream. And we don't notice that the character doing the seeking is part of that illusion, part of that dream.

We don't notice that any knowledge gained from within the dream can only ever be more dream, more illusion. We compile and store and savor our knowledge, begging for more, craving for that one little nugget that might just set us free.

Yet all words, all knowledge, all understanding within an illusion can never be anything but more illusion.

We don't notice that the body which we take as our place of residence is nothing more than bundles of passing sensations experienced, then conceptualized as 'my body'.

We don't notice that mind is only a concept, thoughts are nothing other than sensations over which we have no control; so we're pulled along by thoughts, kicking and screaming and grieving and suffering, identifying as the author of thoughts.

We don't notice that any benefit or special spiritual states can only be more of the same, only passing parts of the dream.

We don't notice that there is literally nothing we can do, because there is no doer.

We're left with nothing to hold on to, nothing to grasp, nowhere to go for answers, no truth hidden between the lines, no reality waiting to be uncovered, no enlightenment waiting to be attained.

We're left in the absence of worldly knowledge, in the direct realization that nothing knowable can be it, everything learned is only illusion.

We're left in the immediate recognition of not-knowing, of not ever able to find an answer, never able to figure it out or come to any completion in the mind.

We're left in pure and simple not-knowing.

Nothing in the appearance can bring the answer. No word can ever describe it. All words only serve to separate, to conceptualize, to create the very illusion from which we were seeking answers, to create the very idea of a seeker.

We reach the edge of the cliff, hanging on for dear life, only to find no cliff and no one that is hanging.

Non-duality points clearly and consistently to the fact of your beingness. Being. Be. Just Be.

And in *Just Be* there isn't anything which can go out and find, attain this or that, become something better or more spiritual or more enlightened.

Just be as you are. Now. No thing, in which all things come and go. No thing, which contains all things. No thing, which is pure experiencing, experiencing which includes both experiencer and experienced, seer and seen, hearer and heard, thinker and thoughts.

No thing, which is nothing other than this very moment, this immediacy, this instant-without-a-second. No thing, which is nothing other than the soft breeze against the face, the aroma of cookies, the pressure of gas, the pain of a migraine and the grief of loss.

The mind makes it complicated. The mind makes it difficult, an achievement, something which needs to be done or is needed to become.

There is an apparent process of mental understanding and then confusion and then moments of clarity followed by absolute frustration. Yet through this back and forth of seeking and finding, dropping and discovering, That which you already are is shining, illuminating.

What-you-are is formless, without attribute, without characteristic, without properties, absent of being or not-being, absent of birth and death. It is beyond all opposites and yet it contains them. It is pure absolute reality – watching the dream go by.

Yet we make something out of that appearance, those sensations, those experiences. We call them something, we apply the subject/object equation and they take on a reality that is false, an illusion.

Silent, still, empty knowing is your true nature. It is the simplest and most ordinary reality. Just This. Just whatever is happening. Just a blade of grass or a sunset, a tree swaying in the wind, a bird singing a song. It is just the sensation of breath, the irritation in the nose, the pangs of hunger at dinnertime.

The sensation of this book in your hands.

Experiencing. Not *me* experiencing, not something experienced. Not the subject, not the object, just plain and simple, formless and empty experiencing.

Pure Seeing. Effortless and Immediate Knowing.

Advaita Vedanta calls it *sat-chit-ananda* and this is what you are.

Being/Knowing/Bliss, Presence/Awareness/Love.

Unshakable peace. Boundless Freedom.

You are That.

No Thing.

Part 4 – Dialogues

I am free from the three kinds of afflictions – those in the body, those from other beings and those caused by higher powers. I am different from the gross, subtle and causal bodies. I am the witness of the three states of waking, dream and deep sleep. I am the very Self, indestructible and changeless.

- Adi Shankara

Can a Thought SEE?

Q: Can a thought see a thought? Or is it the awareness (what I am) that sees the thought?

A: A thought has no power or independent existence. It is just a pattern of energy. Can the thought 'I see' actually see? Can the thought 'I hear' actually hear? No – awareness sees the thought as another object arising. Thoughts arise within the awareness that you are. Notice this now. Aren't thoughts just energy? If thoughts stop for a moment, do you disappear? That pure awareness is functioning always – seeing is happening.

This is a great question. However, all questions are attempts to solve this apparent paradox by using the mind. The mind cannot do anything, has no power. And the mind is not a problem, except when it is identified as what we are.

Simply notice right now that you are aware, you are present, you exist. Pure awareness is there, always. Thoughts come and go, but awareness never goes. What you take yourself to be (the body, the thoughts) is just another object floating or arising in this presence-awareness. What you have always known as *you* has always been this presence-awareness. The *I* is just another thought and when this arises, partly out of conditioning and partly out of language/communication necessity, it has been mistakenly identified with this sense of presence-awareness.

But what you are is present right now, always has been

and always will be. It is impossible to avoid, as it is the very basis for your existence. You cannot see or know anything without it.

The teaching of Advaita is to know what you are through knowing what you are not. You are not thoughts or the body. There is no person, no separate, independently functioning and controlling *I*.

Negate all that you know, stop the search for just a moment and notice the simplicity of This, with no thoughts, labels, concepts; what is left is nothingness, what you really are.

Nothingness arising as the world.

Does Awareness Leave?

Q: I am hoping you might answer some questions for me. I've been around Advaita stuff for a while now and I find that everything will suddenly be very clear and make sense and then, just as suddenly, it all collapses and I think I just keep missing it – whatever it is.

You mentioned something in one of your blogs about seeing that we are not our thoughts and seeing that what we are is before thinking. I get that. We don't need thought to be.

The body, for me, is another matter. It seems that without this body functioning I can't be aware of anything – including awareness. So, even though there is awareness of the body, that awareness only happens as a result of the functioning of this body.

So, when this body dies, what happens? While I might intuit that I am awareness, it seems that without functioning through this body, I, as awareness, won't be aware of myself.

Did any of that make any sense at all? Just knowing that what I am is awareness has given me no peace or comfort or sense of ease. I still get cranky, worry about my horrible credit and debt, dislike my job, feel fat, get gas, worry almost constantly that I have cancer, take walks, love my wife, think I'm a loser who never fulfilled his potential and on and on and on… So this shit is absolutely no use at all.

I read these articles from other Advaita people who say suffering drops away and there is seeing that there is no me – what the %$#@? I stub this toe, it hurts. I get a fever, I feel horrible. Suffering is still alive and well here. So what if I'm just awareness watching it all arise in open space – it still feels horrible. What in the world am I missing?

95

A: You say: 'I find that everything will suddenly be very clear and make sense and then, just as suddenly, it all collapses and I think I just keep missing it.'

Does awareness ever collapse? Can you ever miss or lose awareness? Awareness is the basis for knowing any collapse, any miss, any loss.

You say: 'It seems that without this body functioning I can't be aware of anything – including awareness.'

You aren't aware of awareness. Awareness is. Awareness is what you are. The activity of knowing is what you are. You have never thought a thought, never stubbed a toe. What you are has never gotten cranky, never felt fat, never felt anything. It has only witnessed the body-mind apparently having all sorts of experiences. What you are has been apparently looking out the eyes your whole life. All the while you've been wrapped up in the anxiety, moods, life story, the identification with the body-mind, the belief in the person, has seemingly obscured your true nature. But in reality it is your true nature that enables any of this to be known.

Just relax – what you are is in full view right now. It isn't hard to know but literally impossible to avoid. It is That by which you know anything.

How To Stop Identification

Q: *I have just been reading from* Gleanings from Nisargadatta *and I came across this:*

'You must have full confirmation that You are not the body. This must be firmly felt otherwise it is difficult to pursue this knowledge.'

Was this true for you? This has been troubling as I can see there is identification with this body sitting here typing. How to stop that identification? Please tell. I had thought that as things became clearer, so to speak, that this body thing would take care of itself.

But Nisargadatta seems to be saying otherwise.

A: The root problem is the belief in the separate entity existing in the body. Once this has been investigated and seen as false, how can you be the body?

The teachings use *neti-neti*, not this, not that, as a pointer. *neti-neti* means that anything observable, anything perceivable or conceivable, is not what you are.

So we eliminate anything that appears, including the body and thoughts, as not what we are. In this, we come to see this clear empty witnessing consciousness that is not an object, but is the constant behind every object.

As these words are typed, it is clear that the hands are typing, the body is active. But what is the body? How can I define body or mind or anything unless I go into thoughts, go into knowledge of what has been learned about bodies, or memories of a past body which appears in this moment, now, now, now. There is simply no *me* in any of it.

All there is, is This, in the immediacy of this moment. Anything else is mind only. Right now you are the whole of it, every single bit of it. To say you are the body is a learned belief only. There is no separation. Just This. Anything you can say about now, defining a body, labeling a person, is only mind.

You cannot get out of *now* and cannot go anywhere that is not *now*. And if *now* is the only thing that exists, how can you be the 'George' in that body? There is no such thing.

This teaching is like a virus. It seeps in and works, changing the very way you look at the world. As you begin to question your beliefs and start to see the falseness of concepts, you will see that there is no one there doing any of it and never has been.

Just relax and start from the fact that you already are what you seek. This isn't about gaining anything new, achieving or attaining some blissful spiritual experience. Those may come but they always pass.

This is about looking deeply into what is going on right now. And right now there can be no George.

Q: Thank you so much.

What really grabs me about the way you write is when you say things like:

'How can I define body or mind or anything unless I go into thoughts, go into knowledge of what has been learned about bodies, or memories of a past body which appears in this moment, now, now, now?

98

Unless I go into thoughts. Unless I go into thoughts, go into knowledge. That going into the thoughts part of it... I can feel the impact of it but it hasn't totally sunk in.

I feel the importance of seeing that. So I have to go into thought or go into what I have been told, or go into past conditioning to come out with I am the body.

A: Another way to look at it, from the perspective of the body, is to realize that every single cell that makes up the body has been replaced thousands of times during the lifetime. The very body that is seen is not the same body as 5 or 10 years ago. Where can an entity exist in such a temporary shell?

The body is nothing more than the environment, no different than the planet it walks upon, just as a tree is really part of the earth. The substance of the body is made up of the elements, air, the food eaten. And the food eaten is also part of the earth. The common denominator is life itself, living energy, intelligence-energy. Just as the original cell was the combination of sperm and ovum. And where is that original cell now? Was there a separately existing entity or a person in that original cell that started the fetus? If there wasn't one then, when did it arrive? After the fetus grew a brain? Did the soul magically appear in the body then?

Can you see the nonsense of the belief in a person or a soul or a separately existing entity in the body?

This belief is the root cause of all suffering. If there is guilt, anger, resentment, depression, even happiness, there must be some reference point. 'I feel guilty, I am angry, I am happy.' These all refer to an *I*. But where or what is this *I*?

This is the investigation – see if you can find this *I*. See if this *I* isn't just a convention of language that ended up being believed in as real.

And if there is no *I* in the body, what can *you* be? There is still knowing. And in this very moment, which is the only reality there ever is, where is there any room for a person with its life story and problems? All there is, is This, now. Just what is going on in the immediacy of this very moment, before thoughts come in and label and judge and filter and define and bring memories in to create knowledge?

You are the silent, still, empty, spacious knowingness in which all sound, movement and form arise. Just like the sky – clouds pass by, birds fly through, the sun rises and sets, sometimes dark clouds arise and pass. But the sky itself is never touched. You can't actually hold sky in your hands, you can't actually know the sky unless you describe it in terms of its content. But it is the very space in which all these objects appear. You are like the sky – formless and spacious, the background in which all things arise.

Another way to look at it is to see a mirror. Can you see the actual surface of a mirror? Or are you only seeing the content reflected? Even light itself is reflected in the mirror but the mirror is never touched and isn't seen, outside of the contents of the reflection. You are like the mirror, reflecting every object without being the object or being touched by anything that is reflected.

These are pointers to the already existing presence that you are. It is present right now and you don't need to look for it, because you are it. It is not hard to find but impossible to avoid, impossible to get out of. Even if you stop thoughts, can you stop awareness in this present moment?

It is your true essence, not the body or mind which are temporary. What-you-are is like the sky. Sometimes we have stormy mental weather, but it isn't ever a problem unless we call it a problem in the mind. Then we run into the past or future to fuel the story. And that very story is thought happening now.

There is no one there to whom anything ever happens. There is no one home in that body. There is just This, right now, and you are This.

Q: Thanks so much for the pointers.

It all makes so much sense. It just seems like the belief is so ingrained that it hasn't been seen through yet. I have noticed how it seems that the mind will do anything not to see what is right here and so obvious to many of you.

I long for freedom yet am also afraid at the same time.

A: This is the earnestness that Nisargadatta speaks of: we get to a point where there is no turning back. We can no longer look at the world with the same eyes. We sense the truth of these teachings but somehow feel we're missing it or only understanding intellectually.

We are waiting for something to happen. We have some expectation based on reading enlightenment accounts but it is best to drop all this; it only leads the mind down the wrong path.

What you are seeking, you already are. It's present right now. It is the very basis for reading these words. It is not an object but a knowingness, a beingness, aliveness, awareness. The body appears in it, the mind or thoughts appear in it. I am not there yet the *I* appears in it. 'I long for freedom' appears in it. It is the present knowing space in which everything appears.

The only obstacle to this is believing yourself to be a person who is seeking the truth. Seeking is a denial of

what is, in preference for some better future, where *I* will
be enlightened or wiser or understand Advaita or whatever. Clear seeing reveals there never was a seeker at all.
The questions don't suddenly get answered, the truth isn't
somehow deposited for your enjoyment. There never was a
seeker at all. That's the realization.

Right now thoughts are arising, bodily sensations are
arising. Investigate what is knowing these thoughts and
sensations. Just close your eyes and feel that sense of presence in which all appears. No matter if the mind arises. Just
see it as more objects arising in the vast sky of awareness
that you are.

The only problem is what the mind stirs up. Peace is
the essential nature. It cannot be obscured. Thoughts and
beliefs one way or the other do not ever touch this peace.
And this peace is available right now, when thoughts and
beliefs are seen for what they are. And the root thought/
belief is George.

You are not that George.

Meaning

Q: If I may I would like to ask a question. I have read and heard a number of people say that there is no meaning or purpose to life. It just is. Seeking arises from the seeker believing him or herself to be a separate entity and incomplete.

If there is no separate entity then how could anything arise there from? Surely everything arises from the One and, if that is so, then there could be a meaning or purpose that is emanating from the One. I hope I have made the question clear. I would really appreciate your view.

A: Any meaning or purpose can only be a mental overlay on what is, right now.

Time is a concept only. For any meaning or purpose there has to be time and a *me* as reference points. There simply is no time and there simply is no *me*.

Oneness, this immediate presence, is the only reality. And in oneness, all appears to happen. But it is only the mind that creates meanings and purposes. Prior to these creations of the mind, you are That.

The entire point of all the teachings is to be what you are. Identification with the particular is the problem. In giving up mental definitions, it is immediately clear that there can be no separation, except for an imagined person.

A Light Bulb Moment

Q: I enjoyed your blog... particularly the bit about waiting for the story to get better... a light bulb moment – thank you... It really stunned me, the simplicity of that, which for some reason had never hit me before in all my reading and listening to teachers,

A: Yes, it's very simple and that's why it's overlooked. It's always present and never changes, but we focus on the changing mind content as long as we identify with the mind and its conceptual framework of being a person living a life. The pointers are just telling us to look to That which existed before the mental chatter, to look to That which is the silent space in which all this life story arises. There is nothing more to it than that.

Understanding is pure silent knowing. All the suffering is resolved because it's clear that anything that can arise as a problem is only more mind content, referring often to the past or future and always referring to this non-existent separate person called Elizabeth.

In the immediacy of This, this very presence prior to the mind, this very spaceless space in which it all arises, there is nothing that can be said. Only resting in being and watching as it spins its false web.

Q: Thank you so much. A question I have drives me mad. The silent space in which all this life story arises... where does it go on the death of this body? Can I assume it still illumines other bodies?

I get really stuck on the death thing, because the silent space in which all arises, all the sights, sounds and tastes, still needs sense organs to register content. When this body decays there will be no resting in Being....

A: What's actually happening in this moment is the only reality. Anything else is mind only, which is still only happening now. There is no past or future anywhere outside of presently-arising thought. In this arising, there seem to be perceptions and sensations. The mind labels those perceptions as a body, a thought, another person, a *me*.

If we just pause our thoughts for a moment and look, we find we cannot say anything about it. Words are meaningless, except as a way to communicate mind to mind.

Beyond and prior to the mind, all we know is This, some present perceptions and sensations happening that the mind has labeled and conceptualized. This body that will some day die is just a concept. There is no person in there to die. This arising of what's called a body may cease to function, but it's no problem unless the mind is utilized. Even if you're diagnosed with a terminal illness, it's just a concept. To whom is it happening? The attachment to this perception called a body is the cause of suffering. It's an illusion.

Right now, there is nothing you can say about anything. This very moment is the only reality. Where is the body other than a mental concept? Where is death? Where is Elizabeth?

I'd suggest that there is no Elizabeth or Randall, only present awareness/freedom. But this freedom is not something to be attained; it is ever-present and unaffected by our mental efforts to be free. All the mental effort of seeking is like a hamster running on a wheel going nowhere. At some point, the hamster gets exhausted and dies. The very search is a denial of this present moment, the only reality.

But who is to stop the search?

As long as there is the belief in a person, just resting in Being means to stop all searching and recognize that there is nothing to find or nowhere to go. As the mind resists this, inquire why. Why does the mind resist? What does it want? It wants this freedom that is pre-existing but obscured by the very attempt to find it.

In reality you are doing nothing but resting in Being. It is only the mind that says otherwise.

You are the very freedom you seek, you are not a person limited by mental concepts. Just stop, rest in This and recognize this very moment as the only reality, infinite freedom and love. There is nothing to seek and nowhere to go; you cannot ever get out of *now*.

Preferences

Q: Preferences and aversions are something that seem kind of fundamental to all this. They seem to presuppose some entity I to have them, but they also seem to arise spontaneously, apparently in response to conditioning and instinct.

What's troublesome for me is conflicting preferences/aversions. Take these two thoughts:

I need to do X.

I don't want to do X.

According to non-duality (as far as I understand) the I in those two sentences does not exist outside of the thought. But these preferences do arise. When it's all said and done, X is either done or not.

At some point along the way, I picked up the possibly incorrect notion that understanding the illusory nature of the self would take with it these preferences and aversions that could only possibly belong to the I that we just figured out was nothing other than a thought.

Of course my preference would be not to have any preferences :)

Any thoughts on this?

A: Thanks for writing, my friend.

The mind will always have preferences. That is the nature of the mind. But what you are is the silent knowing awareness that sees the mind, good or bad, having preferences or not.

The key is to look for that *me* who has preferences. Is there, or has there ever been, any such thing, other than a thought, a belief? When you say: 'I have a preference', what's really being said is that a preference is being seen. The *I* is added on by language, and it's so habitual that a solid entity is believed to be there representing that *I*.

This *I* is only a charade, a character in a dream. There is simply no one home, no one at the wheel. You are not the body-mind, but there is a false identification with the body-mind, a belief that there has to be someone there to do it. Chuck is a fiction, only a cloud floating by in the vast and spacious sky of awareness.

Things appear to happen as the body-mind moves about apparently living a life. There is no problem with it and no one there to change it. It simply is as it is, however it is.

Question this sense of *I*, this *me*, every time it arises. If 'I am hungry' arises, look to see if you can find the *I* that is being referenced. Hunger may be arising, but where is the one who is hungry?

Watch the mind, watch without judgment, without expectation. Watch the mind's preferences or aversions arise, watch the disappointment or happiness or seeking as it arises. If identification with these thoughts arises, that's fine; watch that identification also. If the feeling arises 'I just can't get this Advaita stuff', witness that also. At some point it may be seen that there is a space or distance between you and the mind. It seems that you are watching it come and go, so You must be beyond it, prior to it. When it is in abeyance, You still are. What You are is already present prior to anything that may happen.

Just rest in this witnessing. Watch as the I-thought arises, watch the suffering always refer back to this *me*. Watch and see if this *me* is a real thing or only a belief, a presently-arising thought.

What you are is like a mirror: the mirror reflects all that happens but is never touched by anything it reflects. The mirror doesn't have a preference for what arises, doesn't resist reflecting some things. It reflects all equally and effortlessly, without preference.

Q: Thanks for the response, Randall.

What struck me the most was this:

At some point it may be seen that there is a space or distance between you and the mind—you are watching it come and go, so you must be beyond it, prior to it.

I knew this, but didn't really grasp how key this was until you brought it up. I know that something hears the thoughts, but reading this reminded me that attention is still primarily focused on thought.

There is a lot of talk about the illusory nature of the I thought in particular. At one point I had an epiphany that all thought is imagination, albeit sometimes useful imagination. It seemed like the thought of 'no me' was really of no more credibility than the thought 'me', they are both ends of the me stick.

In any case, there is still identification with thought here. It's a heavily ingrained habit for sure. I will continue to question this. It's apparent that there is something prior to thought, something that sees thought. It's also clear that everything I ever thought I was indeed only existed as thought.

A: Yes, even the thought 'I am not the mind' is still another thought. The only true statement the mind can make is: 'I don't know.'

The most basic thought is *I am*. Stay in this and watch this *I am* arise. If I ask who is reading these words, you reply 'I am'. Question who is this *I* being referred to. What is it?

What is this *I am*?

Before thought arises to say *I am*, you already are. What you are is prior to this *I am*, upon which all other thoughts are based.

This seeing/knowing is already happening now. It is the background of all that arises, That which reflects this body, thoughts, the world. This seeing/knowing doesn't have to be attained through arduous spiritual practice or figured out in the mind. This seeing/knowing is the actuality now, prior to any seeking or contemplation in the mind; then later mind comes in to claim it and refer it back to the *I am*.

The mind is only a word used to contain thoughts, memories, emotions. Thoughts seem to arise, but the mind is only a conceptual box used to wrap all these functions up for reference. Similarly, the person, the *me* is also a concept, used to contain the appearance of the body and mind. It is another box used to wrap up all the references. The person is nothing more than a concept. But it's become a habit to refer to it and believe it is a substantial and separately existing entity. It has no more reality than the man in the moon. Even science has not been able to find this so-called person by investigating the brain.

Any movement to figure it out in the mind is a movement into the appearance and away from what is being pointed to. Rest in this spacious and silent being-awareness that is already present and the ground for all that arises. It's like the light shining through a projector. The film (mind) moves and has various shapes and sizes, gives color, movement and form to the light, but the substance of the projection is the light.

Habits need not concern you – let them be as they are.

The mind can do flip-flops, sink into confusion or depression, rise to happiness and bliss, but these things all pass. What doesn't pass is the very seeing/knowing, which is there no matter what the mind is doing.

Hitting a Dead End

Q: Recently, in my quest on this pathless path, it seems as if I've hit a dead-end (I know there is no such thing). When I sit with that presence of I am I witness thoughts coming and going as if I'm standing at the bus stop, watching cars fly past me.

In between those thoughts are moments of clarity where there is pure witnessing. No thoughts to taint what is – complete purity! It is much like a transparent invisible video camera registering everything. Or, perhaps it is more accurate to say, it is more like having your face pressed up against a television screen or computer monitor, but the resolution is much better.

All of these descriptions fall short, and I question why I even bother writing them.

I understand that I must go beyond the witnessing, because the witness isn't consistent (as proven when we go to bed every night and experience deep sleep). I know that I am aware of the fact that I slept well last night, or the answer to the question of who wakes up and answers the phone in the middle of the night. Of course there is Awareness – it's not some switch that can be turned on or off, it always is. So, how to go beyond the witness?

Any help that you could provide, I would greatly appreciate it.

A: Thank you for writing, my friend.

It seems the entire process as you've described it is dependent on you doing something more, doing something different to get farther, attain more, deepen understanding, etc. This is false.

You've pointed to the witness, the awareness of all that happens, as that which doesn't change, that which only watches the passing world. This is an important aspect as it helps to break the identification with the body-mind as what you are.

But, as you seem to be seeing, this is still duality. The witness and the witnessed are still separate things. While this may be helpful to break that identification, it's still conceptual.

This is about seeing through words; seeing that all words are only valid within the system of language and have no absolute value. They create concepts and beliefs which solidify and present the world. This gross world is presented to gross senses, but the essence of the appearance is emptiness.

The Buddhist *Heart Sutra* says that form is emptiness, emptiness is form. So all that we see is, in essence, emptiness. The forms are all made of the elements, which are molecules, atoms, quantum field, energy.

So this world, including the body, is a form of emptiness – or nothingness with no solid and separate existence. It's perceived as solid but is simply empty intelligence energy expressing as form – formed emptiness. So the world we perceive is an illusion; it's not as it appears. This field of empty energy is the basis for the atom which combines to create the molecule, then the element, the cell, the organism. Then consciousness comes, followed by the *I am*, and suddenly I'm a person and I have a life and a mission and I can choose to do this and that and I want to find answers and truth and God.

Even the witness of the illusion is part of the illusion. Because if we look through a magnifying glass to see these atoms or look at the quantum field, that's part of the perception, still made of emptiness. The perceiver is still part of this illusion. The very brain and nervous system which operates these gross senses is made of this nothingness, is not really there.

So we see the inherent falseness of words and concepts and forms. We see how the mind uses words to create this world and to get further involved in religions and spirituality to find answers, to find truth. As we discard these concepts as nothing more than formed emptiness, as nothing more than relative labels to label something that doesn't exist, we rest in this non-conceptual awareness.

And even this is a concept which is discarded. If form is emptiness and emptiness is form, then neither one actually exists. There is no one and nothing to stand apart to say that there is form and there is emptiness. It's all one substance, not two.

And we finally discard even the concept of one substance. If all is one substance, who stands apart to say there is one substance? Who knows this one substance, because wouldn't the knower of the substance be also made of the one substance? So we're left with nothing to grasp, nothing to hold, nowhere to stand, nowhere to go, nothing to become, nothing to gain or lose. The bottom has fallen out and we're left with no foundation whatsoever to hang any concepts on, even the concept of Advaita or enlightenment or liberation. It's an annihilation of all concepts, including the concept of J. trying to figure all this out.

So all this seeking and trying to figure out the answers is an exercise in futility. You already are what you seek. No answer can be found, no seeking can deliver liberation or truth, because these are still concepts and are made of nothing except words. Simply rest in this knowingness, this sense of existence, which doesn't require words or concepts to know. This reveals that even the sense of *I am* is impermanent, and it becomes clear through watching without expectation that all words are false and dependent on other words. Beliefs created out of words are also false.

So we're left with nothing at all, simply This. We can't say anything about it. We can't go into words to describe it or figure it out because we're using the very concepts we've seen as illusion. And This, now, is a miracle, because it appears the world is happening; thoughts come and go, but there is nothing there, nothing is happening and there is no one to say or do anything. Any movement towards seeking an answer is one step too many, a movement away from the already-present nothingness.

And J. always was only ever part of the illusion, a dream character, a mirage that didn't know it was a mirage. The mirage doesn't disappear, only we don't keep going back and trying to get water from the mirage over and over. The habit of continually projecting an image of ourselves stops.

Freefall

Q: You say something about awareness itself being a concept. How to let go of that concept?

There's still a looking here, a holding on to the concepts of Advaita.

This freefall, how does it come about?

There's no relaxing here into being awareness, there's still a holding on to something.

Although it is obvious that awareness is always and is seeing/being whatever's happening.

It's hard to put the question into words, but it has to do with letting go, freefall, letting go of the holding onto, letting go of the mind totally, letting go of control.

Is there something to say about this?

It feels like I could never totally let go. Although there's a longing for that at the same time.

I would love to hear your reaction.

A: Hello, my friend.

Everything perceived or conceived, anything perceived through the senses, is part of the manifest world, the world of form. Even the body we see/feel/touch is part of this. Even thoughts are part of this.

The normal state is of identification with the body-mind, identification with that thing which we seem attached to, the thoughts that only we can hear, the movements that seem directed by these thoughts. This bundle of sensations/thoughts/decisions seems to be *me*. And I know it's

116

me because there are thoughts which say it's *me*.

So Advaita is about questioning what we've always taken ourselves to be. Advaita doesn't offer the answer, it only offers the invitation to question our most deeply held beliefs.

And once we begin questioning this, we start watching thoughts to see if they are *me* or not. We start watching the body to see if it's really *me*, or not.

But the answer never comes. It only becomes obvious that if I'm watching the body-mind, I must be prior to the body-mind. So the body-mind is *neti-neti*, not this, not this.

As further thoughts, sensations, identifications arise, we stay in this witnessing and watch them, further realizing that I am not this, not this.

At some point, it may become obvious that what *I am* is only the seeing/knowing/looking itself. The world and body-mind arise and I'm only That which is knowing the world and body-mind but I'm not the body-mind. This is where the identification with the body-mind falls away. It is easy to see that what you are is the knowing.

So: I'm the knowing and there is the world/body-mind. Duality. Still duality. A world and a knower of a world.

So how do I know I'm the knowing only? Isn't this more knowing of something? Even without a form, the perceiver of the world still appears as part of this conceptual framework.

So this is another not-this. *Neti-neti*.

So I'm not the body, not the mind, not the knower/perceiver/witness – what am I?

Any words that arise are immediately negated in this. There is nothing left to say about it, nothing left to attach an identification onto. That rope we were holding onto becomes part of the illusion and disappears in not-knowing.

The world is made of nothingness, no-thing-ness, no thing. Anything we see or say is not it. The underlying substance out of which this world is made is singular, not-two. There is no real separation between that computer and that body, no real difference between these thoughts and that sky. These distinctions are made in mind only.

And even the underlying substance is a concept used to describe, it also appears in thought and is known to arise in knowingness. If all is one substance, then who can stand apart and point to the one substance? Who can show me the one substance? Wouldn't that immediately be two?

What you are is prior to mind, prior to the body, prior to any concepts about what you are.

Now tell me what you are.

Q: *It is impossible to tell who I am, in words!*

But there is a knowing, though, a knowing somehow that there's a seeing. A seeing that cannot be seen.

Clinging to Oneness

Q: Last week during the online meeting in Second Life, it felt as if I was standing on the edge of a cliff staring into an abyss. Though this description falls short, this feeling has been arising regularly the past few days. I don't know what it is that I am missing. Of course the answer is there is nothing that I am missing.

Perhaps I am clinging to the idea of oneness. A few weeks ago we were speaking of the pointer of the mirror; this was rather helpful. In the reflection of the mirror appears the universe, with no independence whatsoever. It is the reflection (or reflecting, more accurately) that is awareness. The universe cannot be without awareness.

I think as you've said or written, it is like two sides of a coin, arising simultaneously – yet they are one. If I have the correct understanding, the idea of Oneness and a mirror, must be discarded then, because it is a concept. Discarding this leaves pure registering/perceiving.

The pure registering is completely untainted by the mind. The mind which acts as a lens is now crystal clear and the light that shines through is now also pure. So in time these moments of clarity where there is only the chirping of the bird, or the ringing of the bell, in time these moments become longer until it is permanent; this unfolding should happen naturally by itself. My gut tells me this is false because it speaks of a future time – I'm not really sure.

If I see through the world for the mirage it really is, then what else needs to be done? I feel like I'm watching a movie unfold naturally, it is all light on a screen. Thoughts come and go like clouds in the sky. I'm living a very calm, peaceful and tranquil life, but in the background there is a terrible hunger that is screaming for freedom.

A: Good to hear from you, my friend.

If all is Oneness, who can cling to it? Wouldn't that very clinger be part of Oneness?

Is there an *I* outside of Oneness who can cling to Oneness?

The mind is still looking for an answer, an experience to validate some accomplishment. This is the very nature of mind. You are not the mind.

Any answer found, any experience occurring, occurs in this consciousness. Any form that arises (thought, experience) is made of the same emptiness. It's already false – already a formed emptiness. Literally any arising is already false and only happening in consciousness, is not separate or different from consciousness.

Consciousness is primary: all happens in this consciousness. Then the *I am* appears, the sense of beingness, existence. Out of this *I am* come the thoughts that 'I am J., I am a seeker, I am looking for an answer, I am suffering.'

So today a spiritual experience happens ('I am having a spiritual experience'). This is happening in this consciousness only and is formed from emptiness. It only exists as a veil of form.

Then a thought arises which may be a thought of clarity or a thought of confusion or a thought of happiness or a thought of suffering. It's happening in this consciousness only and is also formed from this very same emptiness.

Any thing perceivable or conceivable is not it. Because that very thing is made up of consciousness and is a form of emptiness. If anything happens, that's not it.

So even the sense of existence or beingness is some-

120

thing known in consciousness. The witnessing consciousness watches it all, even the sense of *I am*.

So we start identifying with consciousness only, but
isn't that too a concept? Isn't that also arising in This? So
that's not it. This is the essence of *neti-neti*. Not this, not
this.

So I'm not the thoughts, not the body. All these happen
in consciousness only, are consciousness only. But even
consciousness is formed emptiness.

And form is emptiness and emptiness is form. If they
are the same thing, then does either one really exist? Can a
form in the form of thought or a person stand apart from
emptiness and point to it? They would be pointing backwards, like the eye trying to see the eye.

So what's left? What words can we use? What thoughts
are true? What actions produce valid results? What logic
can we use to find an answer?

What experience validates?

Where is there a J. to find or get anything?

You, my friend, do not exist and never have.

All this world, all the thoughts about finding an answer,
are all a play of form and made of nothingness. So it may
go on or may stop but there is no *you* there doing any of it.

Once the illusion is seen through, the mirage still
appears to contain water. But there is no longer a continual going back and trying to quench our thirst. It's
seen through. The one who could possibly suffer, the one
who was searching, the one who was born and will die, is
found to be nothing more than an illusion, a function of
consciousness, itself part of the illusion.

The absolute or *parabrahman* or God or whatever name
we give to the underlying source or emptiness, is what you

are, what I am, what it all is. And that is already what you are, prior to the seeking, prior to the identification with the form of J., prior to the sense of *I am*, prior to the consciousness in which it appears to happen.

Prior, even, to Advaita or enlightenment.

Why Doesn't the Mind Let Go!

Q: If everything is only thoughts, then why does it seem like it's always the same thoughts appearing? It's always the same thoughts about the same thing? Why is this?

I have finally realized that I will never understand anything with my mind. I just want to let go. I just want to stop, what keeps me from stopping?

When I think about the life of this illusional person, there isn't anything that I would want to hold onto, why doesn't the mind let go?

A: Hello, my friend. Good to hear from you.

Where is there a reference point or a self-center to whom thoughts happen? Thoughts happen but if there is no one there controlling or authoring thoughts, what difference does it make what the thoughts are? You are already not thoughts, already not the mind. It is irrelevant what the thoughts are.

If we see the falseness of the *me*, of the self-center, then to whom can any of it apply? To whom does suffering or even happiness apply?

What-you-are simply watches all this happen; it watches thoughts, experiences, the world. The world, including the body-mind, happens in consciousness. Everything perceivable or conceivable is consciousness, nothing exists outside of consciousness.

And even consciousness is only a concept appearing in consciousness. If all is consciousness, is there anyone standing apart to point to consciousness? Is there a self-center somewhere outside of consciousness which is separate and can speak of consciousness or get answers or find truth?

So even consciousness is only a concept. Literally everything that could be perceived or conceived or thought about conceptually is automatically false and already part of the illusion. So if you're thinking it, it's already false. If you get an answer, it's already part of the illusion.

So where do we go? What can we possibly do to find an answer? What can arise outside of consciousness? Is there a William apart from consciousness?

The mind has nowhere to go. Once the mirage is seen as a mirage, we don't continue going back for water. Without a reference point, a self-center, a *me* there, there is no up or down, no inside or out, no birth or death, no eye, no ear, no enlightenment or delusion, no heaven or hell, no truth or lack of truth, no seeking and no seeker.

No William.

∞

The True Nature of No Thing

Seeing is happening and in this seeing, the ideas and concepts and beliefs in me-as-a-separate-person make their appearance, assert their independence, walk across the stage of mind to demand attention.

Looking for what you are, confusion appears at every turn. When it becomes obvious that what-you-are is what is looking, that you are looking 'from' your true nature, then the confusion falls away. For it is impossible to have experience without the experiencing. It is impossible for the world to 'be' without the subjectivity we know as 'I'.

The appearance of the world depends on this pure subjectivity or 'I' – the sensations taken to be self-existing and separate cannot be removed from this subjectivity. Therefore that pure subjectivity 'is', in the immediacy of this moment, all that it reflects. The subjectivity–'I' is the opening in which the reflection called 'world' unfolds.

'I' is always present, always the knowing in any experience.

Without wading through the worldly knowledge of concepts, Self-knowledge is silent and still. And Self-knowledge is the simple knowledge – 'I' is no-thing.

And no-thing appears as the world.

∞

Acknowledgements

I would like to offer gratitude and love to my friends Areti Alexova, producer of *The Urban Guru Café* (http://urbangu-rucafe.com), Jason Swanson, author of the blog *You Are See-ing-Oneness* (http://youare-seeing-oneness.blogspot.com/), and Catherine Noyce at Non-Duality Press, for their help in getting this manuscript in final order. They have helped to make this expression, which spilled out as quite a mess, into a coherent communication of a very simple message.

Discover all that you are not – body, feelings thoughts, time, space, this or that – nothing, concrete or abstract, which you perceive can be you. The very act of perceiving shows that you are not what you perceive.

-Sri Nisargadatta Maharaj

NON-DUALITY PRESS

If you enjoyed this book, you might be interested in these related titles published by Non-Duality Press.

Oneness, John Greven
Awakening to the Natural State, John Wheeler
Shining in Plain View, John Wheeler
Right Here, Right Now, John Wheeler
You were Never Born, John Wheeler
The Light Behind Consciousness, John Wheeler
What's Wrong with Right Now?, Sailor Bob Adamson
Presence-Awareness, Sailor Bob Adamson
Awakening to the Dream, Leo Hartong
Already Awake, Nathan Gill
Being: the bottom line, Nathan Gill
Perfect Brilliant Stillness, David Carse
Life Without a Centre, Jeff Foster
Beyond Awakening, Jeff Foster
I Hope You Die Soon, Richard Sylvester
The Book of No One, Richard Sylvester
Awake in the Heartland, Joan Tollifson
Be Who You Are, Jean Klein
Who Am I?, Jean Klein
I Am, Jean Klein
Beyond Knowledge, Jean Klein
Living Truth, Jean Klein
The Book of Listening, Jean Klein
This is Always Enough, Jean Klein
Eternity Now, Francis Lucille
The Light That I Am, J.C. Amberchele
The Myth of Self-Enquiry, Jan Kersschot

CONSCIOUS.TV

<small>CONSCIOUS.TV</small> is a TV channel broadcasting on the Internet at www.conscious.tv. Certain programmes are also broadcast on Satellite TV stations based in the UK. The channel aims to stimulate debate, question, enquire, inform, enlighten, encourage and inspire people in the areas of Consciousness, Healing and Psychology.

There are already over 100 interviews to watch including several with communicators on Non-Duality including David Bingham, Jeff Foster, Catherine Noyce, Richard Lang, Roger Linden, Tony Parsons, Halina Pytlasinska, Genpo Roshi, Richard Sylvester, Rupert Spira, Florian Schlosser, Mandi Solk, and Pamela Wilson. Some of these interviewees also have books available from Non-Duality Press.

Do check out the channel as we are interested in your feedback and any ideas you may have for future programmes. Email us at info@conscious.tv with your ideas or if you would like to be on our email newsletter list.

WWW.CONSCIOUS.TV

CONSCIOUS.TV and *NON-DUALITY PRESS* present
two unique DVD releases

CONVERSATIONS ON NON-DUALITY – VOLUME 1
Tony Parsons – *The Open Secret* • Rupert Spira –
The Transparency of Things – Parts 1 & 2 • Richard Lang –
Seeing Who You Really Are

CONVERSATIONS ON NON-DUALITY – VOLUME 2
Jeff Foster – *Life Without a Centre* • Richard Sylvester –
I Hope You Die Soon • Roger Linden – *The Elusive Obvious*

Available to order from: www.non-dualitypress.com